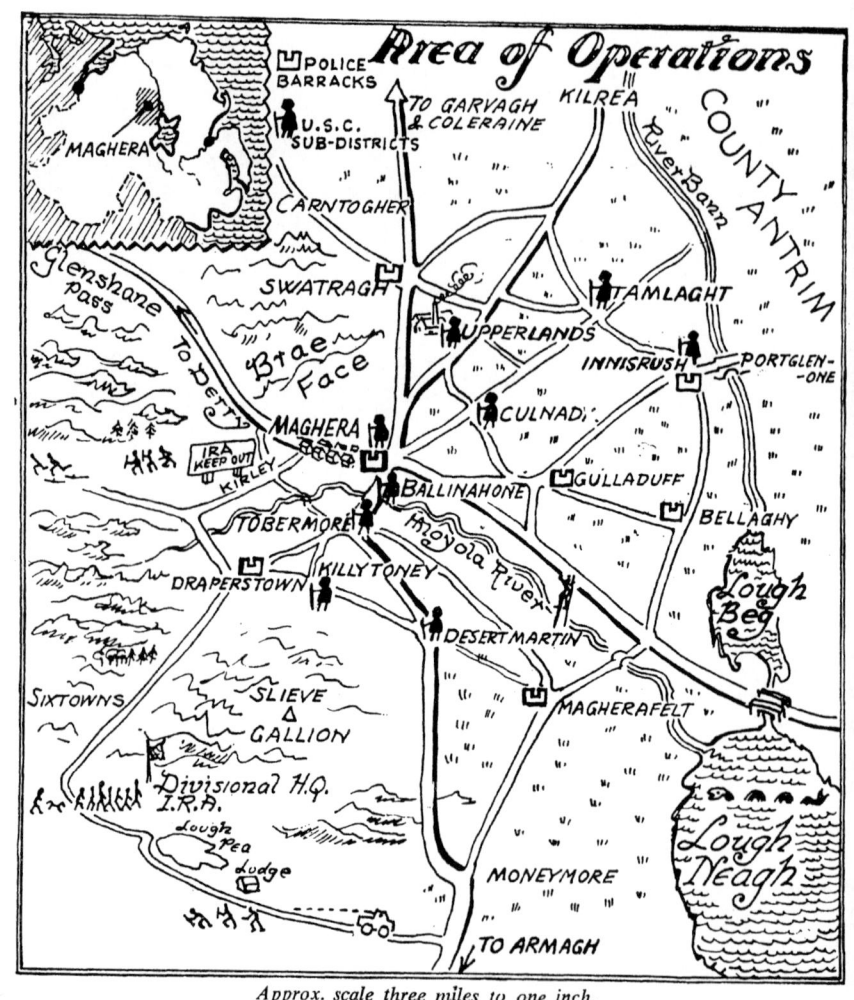

Approx. scale three miles to one inch.

GUNS IN ULSTER

An artist's impression of the ambush of the "A" Specials at the Six Towns

GUNS IN ULSTER

by

WALLACE CLARK

Cover design by Gillian Livsey

Map and line drawings by Richard McCullagh

Published by Wallace Clark   Booksales

**Upperlands, County Londonderry
BT 46 5 SB**

**Printed by Antony Rowe Ltd,
Eastbourne. Sussex**

ISBN 0-9509042-5-2

Copyright Wallace Clark 1963, 2002

Other Books by Wallace Clark
Rathlin –Its Island Story

Sailing Round Ireland

The Lord of the Isles Voyage

Sailing Round Russia.

Linen on the Green
   The Story of an Irish mill village.

Brave Men and True

   Early Days in the Ulster Defence Regiment

FOREWORD

By

The Right Honourable Viscount Brookeborough
K.G., C.B.E., M.C., H.M.L.

I AM delighted to have been asked to write a foreword to Guns in Ulster.

Younger people probably do not realise what the 'B' men have meant to Ulster. Without their courage and devotion to duty, it could well have been that the Province we all love would have perished before it was born.

It was a great experiment and a great risk to arm a civilian population, many of whom had had no training in arms or warfare. Feeling was very high at the time, and such a force could well have lost their heads, and Civil War would have resulted. The provocation was intense. In fact by their innate discipline and sound common sense, under well known local leaders, the 'B' men carried out their dangerous and arduous duties in an exemplary manner.

The story here told is the story of every district in Ulster and their Province owes them much.

BROOKEBOROUGH.

Colebrooke.
October 1966.

PREFACE

IN the following pages all the incidents described in detail relate to one part of Northern Ireland, and many of them to one family. If this method has succeeded in showing in readable form how the tide of national events affected the lives of individuals in three generations, I make no apology for it. Other districts, other individuals may have more exciting or more humorous stories to tell, and if so, I hope that they will record them before they are forgotten. The Maghera district is, I believe, typical and so in the part is best seen the whole.

The warlike events described are still fresh in the minds of those who lived near them. This is not merely understandable, it is inevitable on account of the strong feelings they aroused. Anyone wishing to understand the components in Ulster's outlook today must be aware of this, and of the part the gun has played in her history.

This brief account, the first of its kind, will, I hope, lead to a better understanding of Ulster's attitude and hence better relations with our neighbours.

H.W.S.C.

CONTENTS

			Page
Chapter I	INTRODUCTORY—MEN TO HOLD THE NORTH.	...	9
Chapter II	THE BEGINNINGS OF "THE TROUBLE."	...	15
Chapter III	RAISING THE SPECIALS.	...	27
Chapter IV	THE NORTH FIGHTS ON.	...	42
Chapter V	THE CRISIS OF THE BATTLE.	...	55
Chapter VI	ULSTER GETS HER BREATH.	...	74
Chapter VII	A NEW ENEMY.	...	83
Chapter VIII	SI PACEM VIS.	...	93
Chapter IX	MURDER BY NIGHT.	...	99
Chapter X	PEACE AT LAST.	..	118
	ACKNOWLEDGEMENTS	...	123
	SOURCES.	...	124
	PRINCIPAL DATES.	...	125
	ABBREVIATIONS.	...	127

To the Mothers, Wives and Sweethearts who wait at home.

Chapter 1

INTRODUCTORY

MEN TO HOLD THE NORTH

" I NEED men," said Harry Clark, the forceful District Commandant, " and the younger and wilder they are the better."

He said it in a moment of frustration when recruiting was slow and the need urgent. It was January 1921. Rifles were scarce and equipment scarcer. Newly appointed himself, he was trying to form No. 3 Area, Special Royal Irish Constabulary, County Londonderry, as part of the forces needed to meet the increasing attacks of the Irish Republican Army. These attacks were being ferociously directed against the month-old community of Northern Ireland, a community whose continued existence seemed to be a matter of considerable doubt. Some of the men Harry Clark recruited were wild, but most of them were steady and all of them were deadly determined.

The area in which these men and their sons have since shared with the regular constabulary the responsibility for the preservation of the peace lies between the Sperrin Mountains and the River Bann, or as a local man would say from the Brae Face to the Lough Shore. Three hundred years ago this part of Ulster was known as Glenkonkein and Killetra, the most remote and heavily wooded part of the north, a resort of outlaws, where even the Great O'Neill himself had eventually to seek refuge from the armies of Mountjoy. So it is not surprising that in "The Troubles" of the twentieth century it once again appeared a happy hunting ground for the enemies of law and order.

The mountains to the south and west of Maghera and the localities close to the Bann have been since Plantation days Nationalist strongholds, and in the rest of South Derry, Loyalists and Sinn Feiners are so intermingled that the I.R.A. have been more active here than in any other part of the Province, except for the Border itself which lies as the gunman travels, about fifty miles away. So the Maghera District as No. 3 Area is usually known, has occupied for almost half a century a position of honour where the enemy activity is at times very intense.

The woods of Glenkonkein are all long since gone and South Derry today is a pleasant, mainly agricultural area of small fields and bogland. It is still a key area, for through it pass the main north-south route from Dungannon to Coleraine and the east-west one from Belfast to Derry. Across it flow the Moyola River and several smaller streams, the bridges over which were in 1921 and again in 1956 good targets for the I.R.A. There are three Royal Ulster Constabulary Barracks (or stations as they are now officially called) Maghera, Swatragh and Draperstown, while Bellaghy and Dungiven Barracks lie on the outskirts. In 1921 there were two more, Innisrush and Gulladuff. When terrorists are active these barracks have relied to a large extent on the Volunteers and Specials for protection and the Maghera District has always enjoyed

MEN TO HOLD THE NORTH 11

the most cordial relations with the members of the regular force stationed in them.

Today the Ulster Special Constabulary hereabouts has a strength of some 200 men distributed in eight sub-districts, which extend in the shape of an "L" from Innisrush at the N.E. to Desertmartin in the south. Originally there were five* but of much greater individual strength so that the total in 1922 rose to over 500 men.

The men were originally divided into three categories, the 'A,' 'B' and 'C' Specials. The 'A' and 'C's' have long since been disbanded, and the letter 'B' is officially obsolete, but the name which has stuck is the 'B' men.

A stranger might have been surprised to hear one night in 1938 when a call out was required a girl come running into Sub-District Commandant Clark's study shouting, "Mr. Tommy, yer till scatter the Bees!", but no one in Ulster would have had any doubt as to what she meant!

The members of the District have a remarkable record of continuity of service. In April 1966 one officer and six men who joined between 1921 and 1923 are still serving: S.D.C. John Patterson, S./Sergts. Willie and Alex Crockett of Tamlaght, S./Sergt. Jim Clarke

---

* These were Tamlaght, H/C. Willie White; Culnady, H/C. Wesley Carson; Upperlands, S.D.C. T. J. Clark, H/C. Bob Johnston; Maghera, S.D.C. Dr. R. L. Marshall, and Tobermore H/C. George McDonald. In 1923 Ballinahone S.D.C. McKinney and Killytoney, S.D.C. John Colhoun were added. Desertmartin, S.D.C. Hanna, was transferred from the Moneymore District in 1939. Innisrush, S.D.C. Robert McCaughey, J.P., was formed in 1946 and Ballinahone amalgamated with Tobermore at the same time.

of Tobermore, S/C. Robbie Paul of Maghera, S/C. Jim Millar of Culnady, also P/Sergt. Bob Rainey of Upperlands (who first joined in County Antrim).

The command of the District has been in one family throughout, Mr. H. J. Clark, M.B.E., D.L., J.P., who as early as 1912 had been second in command of the local U.V.F. battalion, was as already mentioned the first District Commandant; to be succeeded in turn by his son, Major Harry F. Clark, M.B.E., J.P., in 1938, and in 1953 by his grandson, Mr. Wallace Clark, D.L., who is still in command. During the war Senator W. M. W. Clark, D.L., J.P., ' old Harry's ' eldest son, commanded both Ulster Special Constabulary and Ulster Home Guard.

Another family of the same name have been S.D.C.s of Tobermore with only a short break since 1922. Mr. John Clark, J.P., was succeeded by his son Johnny, whose brother Andy is now in command of the Platoon.

In Tamlaght, Mr. Willie Clarke was succeeded by his son Robbie in 1931, and another son, Mr. Jim Clarke, B.E.M., was S.D.C. of Upperlands from 1939 until his death in 1956. Mr. John Patterson, J.P., has been S.D.C. of Tamlaght since Robbie Clarke retired in 1940. Mr. Tommy Johnston, J.P., took command of Desertmartin in 1939. Mr. George Mawhinney, J.P., of Killytoney, Mr. Robert Hugh Dripps, J.P., of Culnady, and Mr. Robert McCaughey, J.P., Innisrush, have commanded their Sub-Districts since the 1940s. P/Sergt. J. A. H. Crowe of Upperlands served from 1930-1964 and still attends U.S.C. Shoots and evening functions. S/Sergt. Willie Kincaid and his brother John have been serving since 1930. There are many other officers and men with long service in the District, and the above are only a few examples.

Two of the original officers are still very active today. One is Major H. F. Clark, who became District Adjutant at the age of 17 in 1921, later D.C. as mentioned previousy, served throughout the War in the Army and retired as District Commander in 1955. He re-joined as a S/Con. soon after the I.R.A. started a fresh campaign in December, 1956, became Deputy District Commandant in 1958 and resigned when things became quiet in July, 1962.

The other is Professor R. L. Marshall, M.A., LL.D., D.D., F.R.Hist.S., J.P. He was Presbyterian Minister and first S.D.C. of Maghera and his name still appears on each District Nominal Roll for he is one of the very few honorary officers in the force. An elderly ' B ' man recently recalled Dr. Marshall in April 1922 striding through the I.R.A. camp in Kirley unarmed. " He wasn't feared of anything," he said.

These special circumstances and traditions mean that Maghera have always looked on and conducted themselves as a District second to none—one in which it is a privilege to serve or to have served.

The tradition of long service runs right through the Ulster Special Constabulary, for Col. Sergeant, D.S.O.. M.B.E., was the very well loved head of the Specials from their first formation until a few months before death in 1947. Mr. Jim Harvey, O.B.E., the present City Commandant of Derry, joined in March 1921 and is looked on with pride as the " Father of the Force." D.C. Wilbert Harris of Moneymore as a Head

Constable in 1921 recruited the District immediately to the south of Maghera which he still commands today.

The following pages are not intended to be an exhaustive record, or to dig up the memory of " old unhappy far off things " but rather to tell of some of the good comradeship, humour and unfailing keenness which have been the hallmark of the ' B's ' and the U.V.F. before them throughout their history.

SPECIAL CONSTABULARY.
COUNTY OF LONDONDERRY.

Notice is hereby given that their Excellencies the Lords Justices and General-Governors of Ireland have approved of the application to the County of Londonderry of the Memorandum regarding the enrolment of Special Constables in Ireland, and that Justices of the Peace for the said County have authorised enrolment of Special Constables under the authority of the Special Constables (Ireland) Act, 1832, and subsequent enactments and Orders in Council.

All law-abiding citizens between the ages of 21 and 45 are invited to apply for enrolment for the purpose of assisting the Authorities in the maintenance of order and the prevention of crime in the County.

Applications to enrol may be made on or after the 29th of November, either personally or by letter, at the Police Station most convenient to the applicant's residence. The conditions as to service, pay, compensation, and organisation of the Force are as set forth in the annexed schedule.

    R. SPENCER CHICHESTER, Deputy Lieutenant of the County.

    ERNEST CLARK, Assistant Under Secretary for Ireland.

    C. G. WICKHAM, Commissioner of Police for the Division.

Dated this 27th day of November, 1920.

CHAPTER 2

THE BEGINNINGS OF "THE TROUBLE"

*The dark eleventh hour draws on and sees us sold,
To every evil power we fought against of old.*
From "Ulster" by Kipling

The events leading up to the formation of the Specials were simply those which led to the creation of Northern Ireland. The Six Counties were born under fire, and have been periodically under fire from the I.R.A. ever since, so the Ulster Special Constabulary have remained an essential part of the community.

From the middle of the 19th Century, the British Government had been under pressure from the Irish Nationalist M.P.s who sat at Westminster to grant Home Rule to Ireland. In the view of loyal Ulster this could only mean that they would be outnumbered, three to one, by the anti-British population of the rest of the country; they would lose their British citizenship and they were not going to allow anything of the sort to happen. The phrase " Ulster will fight and Ulster will be right " was coined by Lord Randolph Churchill as early as 1886.

For all this Ireland in the year 1900 was more peaceful and prosperous than at almost any time in her entire history. The Nationalists however continued to press for an Irish Parliament.

It was the Liberal victory in the General Election of 1906 which next sparked hopes for Home Rule. Since the days of Parnell the Irish Parliamentary Party had given the Liberals their support and now an Irish Parliament was looked for as the pay off.

In reply the Unionist Council was formed to fight against Home Rule, and Unionist Clubs all over the country came into existence. The Liberals hesitated.

The year 1911 saw the crisis draw nearer when the Liberals under Asquith found their majority dependent on the support of the 84 Irish M.P.s under John Redmond. Now they would have to pass a Home Rule Bill, not as a pay off but to survive.

Ulster's reaction was swift. She found a great leader in Sir Edward Carson, Q.C., M.P. Seldom in history can any man have commanded such affection and respect or known so well how to use his power. On 28th September 1912, 450,000 Ulster men and women signed the "Covenant" declaring their loyalty to the Crown and determination to use all means that might be found necessary to defend the present constitutional position.

During 1911 and 1912 a good many rifles, mostly ex-Italian Army, were imported by the Unionists but they were of little use without a disciplined force to bear them. The Ulster Volunteer Force was enrolled by a decision of the Unionist Council in December 1912; it consisted mainly of those men who had signed the Covenant and was designed to resist Home Rule by armed force if necessary. In addition a hard core of 2,000 men was specially selected to police the country should the necessity arise, under the proposed Provisional Government of Ulster.

THE BEGINNINGS OF "THE TROUBLE"

Needless to say raising a private army for political purposes was against the law, but the leaders were bold and the cause vital.

The South Londonderry Regiment was raised and commanded by Major W. A. Lennox-Conyngham of Moneymore. He also took charge of the 2nd Battalion himself with Harry Clark of Upperlands as his second in command, while the 1st Battalion C.O. was Mr. Charles Stronge of Lizard Manor. Flagpoles were erected on prominent hills to form a signalling network all over the area. A red flag meant " Report at once with your rifle." One was at Mayagoney and another at Drumoolish, hills on either side of Tamlaght.

Next summer the Rev. John Donnelly who was the very active head of the U.V.F. in Innisrush, wanted to hold his usual Sunday School Sports, but the children would have to march through the Nationalist area of Claudy, and since some might be waving Union Jacks, trouble could arise. On a previous occasion at Castledawson several children had been badly injured on just such an outing when attacked by Hibernians, twenty three of whom were afterwards sentenced. The Rev. John got in touch with Harry Clark and suggested an escort from the Innisrush and Tamlaght companies. Harry thought very highly of the Rev. John and readily agreed though the U.V.F. had as yet scarcely anywhere appeared in public under arms. If the police got word of the idea and arrived in force, there would be trouble of another sort.

Many of the details of this day, which was looked on

locally as a famous one, are now obscure. Alex Crockett (who is still serving in the U.S.C.) recalls that aged 12 he was cutting hay with his father when he saw a man running over the fields. He knew that Sports were on in Innisrush and had hoped to get time off to go to them but now his father said he must finish the hay and take the horses home himself. An hour or so later he saw the Tamlaght men march off, their long bayonets glinting in the sun. They wore Australian style slouch hats, pinned up at one side, and bandoliers across their chests. Harry Clark followed the column with reserve ammunition in his car. They were ready to fight if it came to the point but before getting to Innisrush unfixed their bayonets. The Royal Irish Constabulary were there in some strength at the Barrack (now McDonald's Garage) and senior officers were present. The U.V.F. halted opposite them, turned into line and ostentatiously fixed bayonets. It was a tense moment, but the R.I.C. had a hundred years of experience of this sort of thing and knew when to turn a blind eye. The children assembled beside the Volunteers, and proceeded to march through Claudy escorted by armed men before and behind, though 'tis said that in spite of this some Nationalist women stoned the procession and broke the skin of a " big slapper " drum!

Up until that day the public had credited the U.V.F. with being armed with nothing more than ash plants. Now they knew the truth. The chips were down!

The Ulster Special Constabulary have something to be proud of in being directly descended from the U.V.F. for no finer part time force has ever been raised. The

THE BEGINNINGS OF "THE TROUBLE"

Special Correspondent of the Yorkshire Post, an impartial observer, at a big inspection in Antrim in July 1913 described it as follows:

" As far as I could detect in very careful observation, there were not half a dozen of them unqualified by physique or age to play a manly part. They reminded me more than anything else—except that but few of them were beyond the best fighting age—of the finest class of our National Reserve. There was certainly nothing of the mock soldier about them. Led by keen, smart-looking officers they marched past in quarter column with fine, swinging steps, as if they had been in training for years. Officers who have had the teaching of them tell me that the rapidity with which they have become efficient is greater than has ever come within their experience in training recruits for either the Territorials or the Regular Service."

There must have been many other incidents locally at this time but none are remembered. A scrap of poetry. . . .

" But when the Clarks they heard of this, being in their bed,
They soon arose, put on their clothes, and to Ahoghill sped."

may recall one, but no one seems to know the rest of the verse.

In January 1913 the Home Rule Bill to set up a Dublin Parliament passed through the Westminster House of Commons. Even if held up by the House of Lords it would still become Law in mid 1914.

Civil War seemed very near indeed.

By March 1914 County Derry had four U.V.F.

Battalions numbering 5,360 men, while Derry City's strength was 3,475.

On 16th April 1914 an important ceremonial parade took place in Garvagh inspected by Sir Edward Carson in person accompanied by General Sir George Richardson, the G.O.C. of the U.V.F. and Captain James Craig, M.P. (afterwards Lord Craigavon). Fifteen hundred men paraded in nine companies.*

Sir Edward had stayed the night at Spring Hill, Moneymore, and Alex Clark, D.L., J.P., Harry's elder brother, brought him from there in his Minerva car. This was driven by chauffeur Tom Lamont, later one of the first men to join the Ulster Special Constabulary and still "rarin' to go" today. Tom's son-in-law, Jim, was wounded during the I.R.A. attack in Swatragh in 1958. Such are the family ties in the force.

The cars were carefully routed via Kilrea to avoid the Nationalist town of Swatragh, and were escorted by motor cycle outriders, among them Wilbert Harris of Moneymore and Harry Clark's son Willie.

Eleven nursing centres had been prepared in South Derry, one of them at Ampertaine, Alex Clark's house in Upperlands, and some of the ladies who had volunteered for this work paraded in uniform also.

As usual there was a touch of comic relief for after the parade it was found that the Minerva had gone off with General Richardson's hat and as the General was

---

* These were commanded as follows:
Tobermore, Mr. George McDonald; Maghera, Mr. W. Crogan; Upperlands, Mr. Tom Boston; Tamlaght O'Crilly, Mr. T. Sweetnam, Mr. George Crockett; Magherafelt, Mr. W. Averill; Moneymore, Rev. W. Hogarth; Ballyronan, Rev. F. H. Kinch; Kilrea, Mr. C. Esdale; Innisrush, Rev. John Donnelly.

due at another parade at Drenagh, Limavady two hours later there was considerable consternation until it was found.

The U.V.F. by now totalled 85,000 men complete with mounted units, signallers, and a medical service, but only one in four had a rifle. The Customs were thoroughly on the alert and the smuggling of arms by normal freight had become almost impossible.

A week after the Garvagh parade police intelligence reported unusual activity on the part of the U.V.F. but failed to find out what it meant. Even among the Volunteers themselves few were in the know until the last minute, but by next morning the Force was armed!

The gun-running in Larne on 24th and 25th April was a brilliantly organised operation under the control of General Sir William Adair, while the ship named the Mountjoy was commanded by Colonel Fred Crawford, who had signed the Ulster Covenant in his own blood. Mainly by his personal ability and determination he brought the ship through a blockade set up by the Royal Navy, and landed 20,000 modern Steyr Rifles, made up in fives, complete with ammunition, and ready for instant use. These were distributed by a fleet of private cars from all parts of the Province, and the Maghera Area got its share, 500 approximately. Harry Clark's car met another loaded with rifles at the Hillhead at 3 a.m. on the night of landing. The Castledawson R.I.C. Sergeant was suspicious at seeing the car parked at this late hour and approached, but was beckoned over by Bob McClintock, the driver, and told to sit in the back and ask no questions, which he did. Some rifles were hidden temporarily in Lisnacree Bog.

Ardtara, Harry Clark's house, was a distributing centre and his wife acted as U.V.F. Postmistress. This was a highly organised system extending all over the country as the U.V.F. made no use, for good reasons, of normal postal services, and relied on the same despatch riders as had escorted Sir Edward. Several volunteers, Dan Scott of Upperlands among them, slept at Ardtara to guard the guns until they were distributed.

Some of the U.V.F. had little military knowledge, but made up for the lack of this with enthusiasm. When an Upperlands patrol met a Tamlaght one at Killymuck, each anxious to impress the other with their new rifles, George Crockett of Tamlaght was heard to give his special version of the order to move off; "By the right, left, Quick March!" Another commander used to halt his men with "Whoa."

Meanwhile the Irish Volunteers, forerunners of the I.R.A. were training and arming in the south.

By July 1914, the Ulster crisis was so serious that the British Government ordered naval and military reinforcements to move into the Province. At the Curragh Camp 57 officers, including General Sir Hubert Gough asked to be allowed to resign rather than move to Ulster unless they were assured that no military action against the Unionists was to be ordered.

The Irish question, however, as had so often happened was overshadowed by great international events. In July the Archduke Ferdinand was shot in Sarajevo, and the Great War began a month later. The Home Rule Bill, though passed on 8th September 1914 was

THE BEGINNINGS OF "THE TROUBLE" 23

shelved, with a promise to the South Irish M.P.s that it would be implemented after the war. The men of the Ulster Volunteer Force fought for England and the Empire in France, mainly in the Thirty-Sixth Ulster Division and acquired in the words of Sir Winston Churchill, " a reputation for conduct and devotion deathless in the military history of the United Kingdom." The hospital supplies so carefully assembled in Ulster went to help the Red Cross at the Front.

Many South Derry men were trained at Finner Camp near Bundoran, and most of the rifles smuggled into Larne went to arm the Division which accounts for the comparative rarity of these weapons today.

In 1916 came the Dublin Rebellion, but there was no trouble locally connected with this for although the rebels had dreamed of a general rising and help from Germany their plans were ill laid and the brave men who took over the Post Office and other public buildings in Dublin fought and died unsupported. Harry Clark was in Milford in Co. Donegal fishing when the news came through and drove back at high speed expecting to find the country in an uproar. A hundred and thirty trout the product of a record week-end's fishing were hastily put in the back of the car in brown paper parcels, which promptly burst, and the passengers still remember the misery of sliding round for three hours knee deep in fish as the car bounced over the rough narrow roads.

Within weeks of the end of the War, the I.R.A. not content with the fact that the Home Rule Bill had been passed, stepped up their campaign of violence.

The Soloheadbeg ambush in Co. Tipperary in January

1919, when two policeman were shot dead, was the curtain raiser.

Trouble increased rapidly. In April 1920 Sir Basil Brooke, M.C. (later the Right Honourable Viscount Brookeborough, K.G., C.B.E., M.C., H.M.L., Prime Minister of Northern Ireland) was staying in Dublin and witnessed a strike called by the I.R.A. to force the release of a number of prisoners held awaiting trial in Mountjoy jail. The cases could not be heard since the witnesses had been intimidated and dared not come forward, though many would have liked to do so. Sir Basil saw the spectacle of loyalists forced to conform to the wishes of the I.R.A. against their will and realised that the rebels, having reduced the population and police in the south to near impotence, were already starting to work on the northern counties. He knew that time was short if the loyalists in the North were to combine to protect themselves.

Soon after his eldest son was born on 18th April 1920, he and his wife returned to Fermanagh and then in his own words, "*I stumped the County, explaining the vital necessity of having some organisation, if loyalists were not to be terrorised as in the South. Such was the response that by the autumn, we had about 200 men, and Co. Tyrone under General Riccardo followed suit. We were very sketchily armed, with old Italian rifles of the U.V.F. days and shot guns, but we sat up voluntarily, watching the I.R.A. building up an organisation. We could not do very much, but we caused uneasiness in their ranks and we operated at a moment when the regular R.I.C., after terrible tribulation in the South, were more or*

THE BEGINNINGS OF "THE TROUBLE"

less confined to barracks after dark, and were unable to prevent any terrorism.

"This then was the early start of the Fermanagh Specials, and I am still convinced that without them, Ulster Loyalists everywhere would have been overwhelmed.

"There were of course, a number of stories of the time. I always think one of the best was the moment when I visited a patrol at about 2 a.m. They promptly presented arms. I said nervously, "You don't pay compliments after dark!" One man continued to present arms, with a double-barrelled shot gun with both hammers up! I said, "Put down that gun quietly. It is very dangerous!" "Aye," said he, " I think I will; she's a kind of aisy on the let aff!""

By late 1920 the U.V.F. had been reformed under Colonel Sir Wilfred Spender, K.C.B., C.B.E., D.S.O., M.C. but there were many gaps in the ranks. Tom Boston for one, the Upperlands Company Commander, had been killed in France in 1917. The U.V.F. engaged the enemy on several occasions, still having however, no legal right to carry arms and having to hide at the sight of a police patrol unless the individuals in it were known to be well disposed towards them. Fierce rioting took place in the cities, 60 people being killed in Belfast in 1920, while in June that year the I.R.A. attempted to take over the whole of Derry City west of the river. Twenty civilians were killed by indiscriminate sniping before the Military were called in and armoured cars proceeded through the town machine-gunning the terrorists, some of whom had posted themselves in the trees along Bishop Street. No

I.R.A. casualties were admitted but next morning a local undertaker got a record order for fifteen coffins!

The state of Ireland as a whole may be gauged from the following figures. During the year 1920, 75 courthouses were destroyed, 26 R.I.C. barracks were captured and destroyed and 518 others burned after vacation, 193 policemen and 52 soldiers were killed. Girls who walked out with policemen were beaten and had their hair shorn off. Men considered to be informers were shot. In many parts of the country magistrates were ignored and people perforce took their cases to the rebel courts for a hearing, so great was the power of the I.R.A.

Then reinforcements for the R.I.C., recruited in England and known as the "Black and Tans," and a division of ex-officers, known as Auxiliary Cadets, organised in fifteen companies a hundred strong, were raised to fight terrorists in the South, so that by the end of the year the number of arrests and convictions were showing progressive increase.

Ulster with a predominantly loyal population was relatively peaceful, but "They were bad times," as an old Culnady 'B' man recalls. "No one would have opened the door at night unless he was sure who was knocking, or gone out alone after dark even if in bad need of the Doctor. We just used to ambush ourselves along the road and try to protect the police barracks."

Against this stormy background Northern Ireland was first formed as a political entity.

Chapter 3

RAISING THE SPECIALS

*"We asked no more than leave to reap where we had sown,
Through good and ill to cleave to our own flag and throne."
From "Ulster" by Kipling.*

In December 1920 Lloyd George's Government of Ireland Bill, which is still Ulster's Constitution, became law. Partition was created as yet another bid for peace in Ireland. The I.R.A. in reply promised to shoot anyone who stood for the Northern Parliament.

Those who had boldly but unofficially undertaken the task of maintaining security by reforming the U.V.F. now saw the need to put the Loyalists of Ulster into a position where they could help the Crown Forces. Sir Basil Brooke visited Sir John Anderson, then joint Under Secretary to the Lord Lieutenant in Dublin Castle, and forcefully pointed this out. As he recalls:

"We soon realised that it was essential that our entirely voluntary and unofficial force should be recognised by authority. It was however only after strong opposition that Sir John Anderson was persuaded of the necessity. They did not at all realise the danger of our activities, opposing armed and ruthless I.R.A. as we were, and the first order authorising our formation, but issued only with armbands and whistles, caused immense merriment in Fermanagh when I conveyed it to meetings in the County."

The scheme which Sir Basil and his associates had pressed differed little from that eventually adopted.

In September 1920 the Belfast Branch of the Secretariat under Sir Ernest Clark sponsored the recruiting of the official armed Force. On 22nd October the details were published and read as follows:

" The scheme, which applies to the whole of Ireland, will be brought into operation area by area as circumstances may require. The first Class of Constable is Class A—that is to say a whole-time man enlisted to serve on the regular Royal Irish Constabulary but only within the divisional area wherein he is recruited. These men get uniform, quarters (or an equivalent rent allowance), pay at 10/- a day, and sundry other allowances, making a total weekly pay of £3 17s. 6d. Arms and equipment will be similar to those borne by the Royal Irish Constabulary.

Membership of Class B entails occasional duty, usually one evening a week exclusive of training drills, in an area convenient to the member. Day duties will not be required except in emergency. These services will be unpaid, but a £5 allowance will be paid for each six months of service, to cover wear and tear of clothes and boot-leather.

Caps and Armlets will be provided, but arms and equipment will be determined by the authority of the county. They will usually be the same as those borne by the regular police of the district at the time. For each drill attended in excess of one per week, 2/6 will be paid. This class will be under its own officers, but these will be under the police authority of the area in which they serve.

Class C is a reserve. Members will serve in a

district convenient to themselves, and will be called on only in case of an emergency. They draw no pay or allowances and do only occasional drills."

The scheme was brought into operation by pairs of counties. Derry and Antrim together were a week or two later than those on the border and the Proclamation calling for recruits there was published on 27th November 1920. It was signed by Sir Ernest Clark, Colonel Wickham, the R.I.C. Divisional Commissioner (later Sir Charles Wickham, K.C.M.G., K.B.E., D.S.O., first Inspector General of the R.U.C.) and R. S. Chichester, exercising one of the rarely used responsibilities of a Deputy Lieutenant " to raise a Militia."

The I.R.A. liked the Specials no more than the M.P.s and promptly issued a bulletin describing them as a body of murderers and threatening death to anyone who joined. This announcement caused little concern in Ulster. By early 1921 many units of Specials had already been formed and there were platoons of 'A' men in many parts of the country, including Magherafelt,* Dungiven, Derrynoid near Draperstown and Claudy. The 'A' men were trained at Newtownards.

Sir Basil Brooke became first County Commandant of Fermanagh.

---

* The Magherafelt Platoon No. 14 was formed on 28th February 1921, and first commanded by Lieut. A. Young; he was demoted to 2nd in Command of No. 1 Platoon, Kilkeel, and Lieut. Munn, afterwards Adjutant of Derry County took over. They lived in the Workhouse, now the Mid-Ulster Hospital, and Lieut. Barr was 2nd in Command. A handsome and plausible young officer known as "the symphony in brown" commanded Derrynoid. He had a wife and children in England, but after dining one evening with a local landowner, eloped with his host's daughter!

Colonel George Moore-Irvine was Londonderry County Commandant with F. W. Jones as his Staff Officer, and his Headquarters first at Victoria Barracks, later St. Columb's House, Londonderry. Bill Bennett was Paymaster, later to become Assistant Staff Officer up until 1959 for the whole U.S.C. It was not until several years later that the City and County became separate units.

On the I.R.A. side it was the Second Northern Division which occupied most of County Derry and a large part of Tyrone, with No. 4 Brigade on the North West and No. 3 on the South East, the dividing line running just south of Maghera, through Brackagh, Gulladuff and Lislea. Divisional strength in July 1921 was 2,800 men.[*]

The I.R.A. Commandant in Maghera was a man of considerable ability, Dan McKenna (Donald), who at that time was a barman in McKenna's pub. Dan Donald, to give him the name he was known by, became in turn Battalion, Brigade and Vice-Divisional Commander. He later joined the Free State Army and as a Colonel was a member of the Military Tribunal responsible for the arrest of many of his old comrades, when the Dublin Government were in conflict with the I.R.A. He eventually became Chief of Staff with the rank of Lieutenant-General and was responsible for the defence of his country throughout the 1939-45 War. On his retirement as a General in 1948 he was Guest of Honour at an Army Council Dinner in London at which General Sir Gerald Templar, General Sir James

---

[*] " No Other Law," O'Donoghue.

RAISING THE SPECIALS

Steele and other senior British Officers were present. One event which is said to have taken place in Dan Donald's early career gives an indication of his courage, although the details with the passage of time are somewhat obscure. A box, which purported to hold groceries was delivered to Maghera Railway Station and addressed to Patrick McCormick, Grocer, Ballynure. The box contained a Thompson Sub-Machine Gun and was collected by Dan Donald. The authorities were informed and two Crossley loads of ' A ' Specials from Magherafelt decided to capture him and the gun. He was overtaken on the Quarter Road, but made off into Tirnoney Rocks, from where he held off the entire force and eventually escaped taking the gun and ammunition with him.

Such was the stormy background when in January 1921, Harry Clark was appointed District Commandant of Maghera. He was a man of enormous energy, widely respected and liked, for he had the happy knack of treating every man the same from the youngest recruit to the Lord Lieutenant. He was also a forceful speaker and promptly organized a series of public meetings to raise recruits. It was known however that few rifles, little ammunition and no uniforms were available, so men were slow in coming forward. The dates of the smaller meetings are not on record, but the first and main one was in Maghera on 13th January in the Church School.

The County Commandant, D. I. Dudley, D.S.O., Magherafelt, Captain Bailey, County Adjutant, Rev. Maturin, Maghera and Dr. Marshall were present. Harry Clark and the others addressed the meeting and when everything was said that was needed to be said, fourteen Maghera men came forward.*

The Upperlands men had marched in to Maghera behind Jimmy Shiels, playing an accordion. Their first Head Constable was Bob Johnston. He was known as Framer Bob for there were two other Bob Johnstons, "Limer Bob" and "Office Bob," in the Clark's family linen firm, each called after the job they did there! Ernie Lee of Upperlands had been appointed District Clerk and assisted with the swearing in of those who joined.†

When the Police Sergeant objected to Joseph Burns (who has since had a distinguished career of public service and is now M.P. for the area) on the grounds that he was under age, Harry Clark over-ruled him. A second meeting was held a week later when a few more men came forward but Maghera post was so small that for some time it was attached to Upperlands, and there trained in the Orange Hall with wooden rifles which had belonged to the U.V.F. Not much was done in fact until May, when another meeting in the Assembly Hall brought the strength up to 27.

Tamlaght Sub-District was signed on on 21st January 1921, in the Orange Hall in the same way. Willie Clarke, followed by Willie and Alec Crockett, were

---

*These were: Dr. Marshall, William Patterson, Thomas Bradley, Matthew Winton, John McConaghie, Joseph Steele, Joseph Burns, Robert Smyth, Cecil Carr, Robert Shiels, George Shiels, Sam Shiels, and James Smyth.

† Among the first to sign were: Harry Douglas, Jimmy Shiels, Alfred Getty, W. Brady, Sammy Ballantyne, S. Johnston, Sam Forgrave, D. Scott.

Joe Lindsay signed on for Culnady post but the names of the other Culnady and Tobermore first night men cannot be traced.

RAISING THE SPECIALS

the first to sign, and the Rev. Robert McQuaid, the Rector, signed on as a 'C' Special. Desertmartin was signed on on 6th January as part of Moneymore District.

Things remained surprisingly quiet at first and it was not until nearly three months after this that the 'B's' put out patrols, Tamlaght's first being on 7th April. There were only enough rifles for one section per platoon so these had to be drawn from the H/C before going out and returned in the morning. "Some of the boys knew no more about them than a mad dog knows about his father," recalled Alec Crockett. "It's a wonder no one was shot. They were mostly young lads between 17 and 20 and were able to stand up to being out all night from 7 p.m. to 7 a.m. and do a day's work after it." *

In the month of May, the Presbyterian Minister of Maghera, Dr. R. L. Marshall, agreed to take charge of the Platoon there. He divided the 27 men into three sections and asked each man to write on a piece of paper the name of the person he wanted to be his Sergeant. This resulted in Thomas Bradley, William Patterson, and Bob Smyth being promoted and they in turn voted that Thomas Bradley should be Head Constable. Mr. Joe Burns M.P. recalls: "At a meeting held in May in the Assembly Hall, 13 old and practically useless rifles were distributed together with 50 rounds

---

* Seven Tamlaght sections were formed, one for each night of the week. The following were the first Sergeants, J. A. Crockett, W. Davidson, J. Gilmour, John Bloomfield, J. Lennox, J. Doughert. It was Sergt. Crockett's section which carried out that first patrol on 7th April and the men in it were Alex and Willie Crockett, J. Kenny, R. Reid, J. Stuart and W. Kelso.

of ammunition per rifle plus an arm band and a Police cap. Drill nights were arranged and took place every Wednesday night in the old Orange Hall and the men patrolled the roads and countryside seven nights a week. The idea was that one man should do one patrol per week but many times he did two and always at least three patrols a fortnight. It was decided that Cecil Carr, being an Englishman and an ex-serviceman (and incidentally a Roman Catholic) should be given one of the 13 rifles. It proved to be a great mistake. Carr was very near sighted and like the bats had a built-in radar system, which took the form of very acute hearing. It was impossible for him to recognise anyone even at a short distance and he believed that when he shouted " Halt " it was his duty to see that the person addressed was halted permanently. He fired at every sound and was a bigger danger than the I.R.A."

During the spring of 1921 the condition of the country grew steadily worse. Rasharkin Barracks was attacked on 28th January; Gulladuff Barracks was abandoned and promptly taken over by the I.R.A. Many roads were trenched, some by the I.R.A., others by our own side, to keep traffic to main routes. Bridges on Glenshane Pass and in many other places were blown up. The Crossley tenders used by the police carried boards slung under the chassis for use in negotiating these obstacles, but suffered from the great disadvantage of having very noisy engines with a most distinctive note and since motor vehicles of any other sort were comparatively rare they could be identified many miles away. The Magherafelt Platoon was ambushed at the Six Towns, a bomb being thrown right into the

RAISING THE SPECIALS

back of the tender, but got out again by one of the 'A' men before it exploded.

In May 1921 the first General Elections under the new Act were held in the North and South. 'B' men from all over the District patrolled the roads on bicycles and guarded the polling stations for it was expected that the I.R.A. would attempt to interfere with voters. S/C. Sam Twograve was found asleep in the afternoon and had to be taken home. "How could I be drunk?" he protested, "I only had 35 bottles of porter!"

In the South, Sinn Fein candidates were returned unopposed in all but four seats. In the North, a Unionist Government was elected with a majority of 28 and King George V showed great personal bravery in coming to open the new Parliament on 22nd June.

This great event took place shortly after one still talked of in South Derry as the "Swatragh Ambush." Swatragh Barracks had re-opened as recently as the previous March, after twelve months closure. On the evening of Sunday, 5th June, the D.C. was away in Norway on business and S.D.C. Tom Clark was ill in bed. At about 1 a.m. young Harry Clark, left as the senior officer in Upperlands, was sitting with Ernest Lee, S./Sergt Joe Lamont, John McClean and George and Alec Clark, on the parapet of the "Road Engines" Bridge. The Broghan House, down a set of steps close to the bridge, was then and for many years afterwards, used as a starting point for Upperlands patrols. It was normally a resting place for men working the linen beetling engines which were kept going all night. Someone had just remarked that it seemed a quiet night when the patrol heard shooting followed by a maroon or "sound bomb" from Swatragh Barracks. Immediately the Works horn was sounded and the whole Upperlands platoon turned out. They at first bunched round the back of the Lapping Room until "young Master Harry' sent them out in parties round the Works and was himself for setting out direct for Swatragh but was advised first to go to Maghera for support. He and John McClean, with George Clark and Ernie Lee, collected the Maghera Sergeant in the Marmon car and then drove to Swatragh to find that a police patrol had been ambushed in Ringsend at the lower end of the town. A candle had been left burning in a cottage window and 20 I.R.A. men had opened fire from behind a wall opposite, as the police passed the light. If the fire had been properly distributed all three men in the patrol would have been shot. As it was the police fought back fiercely. Sergt. Michael Burke got off four shots before he was killed. Constable Johnny Kennedy was severely wounded with shot gun pellets in his neck. With his wounds bleeding copiously he struggled towards the Barrack for assistance; meanwhile the third man, Constable Anderson got down on the road beside Sergt. Burke's body and replied to the fire of the attackers, thus saving the rifles and ammunition of the patrol. The Police in the barrack would not at first open the door to poor Kennedy but when the 'B's' arrived, they found that the attackers had disappeared while the Sergeant's body lay on the day room table, and Constable Kennedy was apparently dying.

Harry Clark and party drove to Maghera since all telephone lines had been cut to fetch Dr. Kelso who said that only if Kennedy was on an operating table inside half an hour could his life be saved. In spite of the severe risk of a further ambush, Harry Clark, accompanied by Ernie Lee, then drove him to Coleraine Hospital where he was operated on immediately, thereby undoubtedly saving his life. Those in Upperlands had no knowledge of what was going on and had come to the conclusion that the 'B' party had probably all been killed. The Maghera Sergeant sat in the back of the car with a repeater shot gun and during these runs sprayed the windows of the houses in Swatragh as the cars passed through so that the driver thought the firing was coming from the houses. Although already flat out he tried to force even more speed out of the car. Constable Kennedy survived his wounds but almost lost his voice as his vocal chords were damaged. He lived at Carnroe for many years afterwards and was called "Hoarse Johnny" on account of his disability. When the Marmon returned to Swatragh, Magherafelt and Dungiven 'A' Platoons had arrived as also the Divisional Commissioner, Colonel Wickham and D.I. Lester from Coleraine. A sweep was planned for the next morning, and as the Crossleys drove up the Corlecky road a man half dressed was seen running out of the back of a house. He was promptly captured, and another man from nearby as well. Though threatened with instant shooting they refused to give any information. The names of all twenty of the I.R.A. men who took part were obtained by 'B' Special Intelligence during the month or two following the ambush. They were local men led by two from the South and nearly all those concerned met untimely deaths within a few years, one being run over by a motor car in America.

Swatragh was a very different place then in appearance from what it is today. It was almost all thatched cottages, many being roofless and in tumbledown condition. Open drains ran along the two thoroughfares known affectionately as Sheugh Street and Slap Street. In spite of all the rebuilding which has gone on the wall from behind which Sergt. Burke was shot still stands.

The following poem composed at the time commemorates his death:

THE MURDER OF SERGEANT BURKE

Come all you loyal Irishmen,
Who hate this Sinn Fein work,
I'll tell you of that awful deed,
The murder of young Michael Burke,
He was a Police Sergeant,
That done his duty well,
In Londonderry city,
And the district where he fell.

It was in the town of Swatragh,
The bloody Sinn Fein band,
For the murder of the Sergeant
An ambush they had planned.
The Sergeant went on patrol that night,
He had no fear at all,
But he little knew the cowardly horde
Did lurk behind the wall.

'RAISING THE SPECIALS

When passing through Ringsend,
On him they opened fire,
To riddle him with pellets,
It was their chief desire,
The Sergeant stood on self defence,
Of shots he fired four,
Till he received a mortal wound,
And fell to rise no more.

Of all the deeds of cruelty
By savage Hun and Turk,
There is nothing can exceed
This bloody Sinn Fein work.
How can you ever think such men
Would rule our Country right,
That murder brother Catholics,
In the middle of the night?

So now Sinn Feiners stop,
You won't advance your cause,
By shooting down the Police,
Who carry out the laws.
If you have a quarrel against the Government,
Why don't you rise and fight,
The Forces of the Crown,
Will meet you in daylight.

It would be far more honourable,
But you will find it tougher work,
To meet in broad daylight,
Such men as Michael Burke.

*Now come all true hearted Irishmen,
From Country and from Town,
We hope with us you will join
These murderers to put down.*

*And then our Country shall be free,
And Ireland will be blest,
And every Mother's Son of us,
Can go to bed and rest,
Our friends which are at home,
And those across the seas,
Will hail the glorious memory
The rising of the ' B's.'*

Alex Kirkpatrick.

The R.I.C. were again withdrawn from Swatragh shortly after this ambush. Upperlands 'B' men were called on to patrol the village and went there and back on foot.

Young Harry Clark led the first patrol and nerves were taut. Just as they passed the scene of the ambush, a great white shape jumped out at him in dead silence. S/Con. Alec McClean lifted a big stone and threw it at it. The creature fell on the ground . . . it was a white dog . . . struck dead.

D.I. Dudley D.S.O., was at this time in Magherafelt, a man with a fine war record, promoted from the Auxiliary Division, but he got in financial trouble and was arrested. Harry Clark, with his sons, visited him in Derry Gaol, and later helped to secure his release on bail and discharge. It was suspected that he had taken away a U.V.F. machine gun which was in store

The Swatragh Ambush, June, 1921

Maghera Sub-District in 1921

Front Row—Cecil Kerr, Willie Patterson, Dr. R. L. Marshall, T. Bradley, George Shields, T. Steele.
Back Row—Alex. Richardson, Hugh McKeown, Albert Nelson, R. Gibson, Jack McKeown, Tommy Richardson, John Hamilton, Albert Paul.

U.V.F. Despatch Riders Camp, Magilligan, June, 1914.

[R. Clements Lyttle, Photo lent by Rev. Brett Ingram

Crossley and Armoured Car at Ardtara, 1922

A Rolls Royce Armoured Car and a Crossley Tender about to set off on a sweep from Ardtara House, Upperlands, in 1922. Figures, from left to right: Crossley--Standing, John Shiels, Jim Clarke. Sitting, D. Scott, Sandy Farrell, A. Richardson, E. Lee, T. J. Clarke, S/I. Burke.

Armoured Car—R. Scott, John Given, Jimmy Shields and Harry Stewart, Army Driver.

U.V.F. Dispatch Riders Camp, Magilligan, June, 1914.

First Row—........., C. Ross (Lurgan), R. Good (Derry), G. Boyton (Convoy), ..., H. Boyle (Belfast).

Second Row — ...., S. Sloan (Cookstown), ..., ..., ..., W. Shannon (Derry), Major D. Wilson (Killinchy), ..., G. W. Ingram (Ballymote), Malcolm McKee (Bangor), W. Kennedy (Derry).

Third Row—R. C. Lyttle (Belfast), ..., R. Whitsitt (Belfast), Major J. Colhoun, J. Thompson (Belfast), 4 Sayers (Organiser U.S.D.R.C.), J. T. Withers (Belfast), J. Thompson (Belfast), ...

Fourth Row—W. J. Chambers (Belfast), Marshall Kennedy (Derry), ..., P. Bell (Belfast), M. Martin (Belfast), ..., ...

Moyola Bridge After Explosion, 1922

Moyola Bridge the morning after the explosion in March, 1922. Three bombs which were found unexploded in the wreckage may be seen in the inset.

[Photo by courtesy *Belfast Telegraph*

Tobermore Road Post, 1922.

at Moyola Park, on the excuse that it needed cleaning and that this weapon subsequently found its way into the hands of " Trigger " Tom Morris, an I.R.A. officer in Moneymore. This man had also had a distinguished Army career, won the M.M., been commissioned on the battlefield and demobilized as a Major.

Later the same month, Mr. Steele of the Ulster Bank, Maghera on his way to open the Tobermore Branch on Market Day, was captured by the I.R.A. at the point where the Mullagh Road crosses the main Maghera/Tobermore Road. He was put in the back of an open car and driven off towards Glenshane but the hood blew back after a few hundred yards, and the gunmen had to stop to secure it. Steele seized the chance and tossed the notes he was carrying in his pockets over the hedge. The cash box only contained a small amount and the I.R.A. would have almost certainly shot him had they seen what he was doing but later he managed to persuade them to let him go as they retained the cash box which they fancied to be more valuable.

Mr. Steele collected the notes while walking back to Maghera and was very handsomely rewarded by the Directors of the Bank for his action.

Meanwhile the main battle against the I.R.A. in the South of Ireland seemed to be going well. Many gunmen had been killed, others imprisoned; arms and ammunition were in most places very short.

Suddenly to the surprise of almost everyone except perhaps the politicians in London, a Truce was signed on 10th July, 1921.

Chapter 4

THE NORTH FIGHTS ON

*We are closed in —the key is turned,
On our uncertainty; somewhere,
A man is killed or a house is burned,
Yet no clear fact can be discerned.*
In the time of Civil War—Yeats.

By July 1921 some 3,000 people had been killed or seriously wounded in the fighting in Ireland. This was less than would have been lost in a day's skirmishing on the Western Front, but the British people were weary of war. They had also been subjected to extremely clever propaganda by the I.R.A. Their politicians lacked confidence and so it was that the Truce came to be signed. Loyalists in the south who had fought the enemy at risk of life and property found themselves let down by England in a way they had never believed possible. The British Government's main shortcoming had been in its failure to produce any counter propaganda. Irish Nationalist feelings fed on half truths grew fiercer and fiercer until the Irish sceptre fell from England's nerveless hand.

The southern part of the country was now to be ruled by the descendants of those who had conquered it from a previous wave of invaders hundreds of years before. It remains a land full of charming people, delightful to visit and live in when at peace but whether the ordinary Irishman has been any happier or more prosperous as a result of the political change is a matter of considerable doubt.

Many and great injustices in the preceding centuries can be truthfully held against the English in Ireland who had behaved much as any conqueror of the time would have done. Recently for lack of any serious misdoings, they had been blamed for everything from ingrowing toenails to the weather. Now at least the traditional "agin' the Government" attitude of the Irishman could be directed at his own fellow countrymen!

But there was nothing nerveless about Ulster's attitude. She squared her shoulders to fight for as long as was necessary and to co-exist peacefully with the new regime as soon as might be possible.

Meanwhile the Republicans had won a victory of which they had every reason to be proud. The methods used were dirty but no dirtier than those used by both sides in the earlier wars which have split Ireland at frequent intervals throughout her history. Richard Mulcahy, the I.R.A. Chief of Staff and a very brave man, afterwards admitted, "There was not one of us who did not know that the Truce came just in the nick of time—that the War if it had gone on much longer it might have ended in complete collapse." The British Army knew the same.

General Strickland was within days of complete victory in Cork, where I.R.A. activity had been greatest. A young Northern Irishman Bernard Montgomery on his staff recalls that he went almost mad at the news, and walked about for whole nights cursing the politicians. Both sides fully expected negotiations to fail and the fighting to break out again.

The Truce was freely broken, the R.I.C. reporting over 500 occurrences in all during the five months it lasted. The first one locally took place when the ink was scarcely dry on the agreement, on 12th July. It is difficult to make out exactly what happened but according to the papers the Upperlands, Killymuck and Tivaconavey Orange Lodges were fired on while returning from "the Twelfth" celebrations. The Orangemen quickly got rifles and opened up in return but there were apparently no casualties except to livestock. Local tradition says that the Orangemen found something they fancied to be a green flag on their Hall on their return, and some unfortunate animals owned by Nationalists were shot in reprisal.

On 10th October John Buchanan, the Master of an Orange Lodge near Derry was shot dead while returning from Derry in his cart. On 3rd December, during a jail break by I.R.A. prisoners in Derry City, a warder died as a result of being gagged and drugged.

Hard fought negotiations in London dragged on. The Treaty setting up the Irish Free State within the British Empire was signed there in December 1921, but was only ratified by a narrow margin in the Dail and part of the I.R.A. did not agree with its terms. They wanted to fight on for complete independence and now became known as the Irregulars. Led by De Valera they pursued a policy of fierce opposition to the new Dublin Government, and continued the attacks on Ulster. At the same time some of the Regular or "pro-treaty" commanders including

Michael Collins were playing a double game appearing to observe the Treaty in public yet launching attacks on Ulster either independently or in co-operation with the Irregulars. A number of experienced I.R.A. officers from General Liam Lynch's Cork Division were sent north to take charge. Lynch was anti-treaty but in this arrangement Collins and he worked together as closely as in pre-truce days.

Sean Lehane, then O/C. Cork No. 3 Brigade, was sent to command First and Second Northern Divisions, with Charlie Daly of Kerry No. 2 Brigade, who was already in the area, as Vice O/C. Other officers, to the number of about 20, were included in his party. More were to follow, including machine gunners. Attacks on Londonderry were to be mainly based on Donegal.

In April Churchill announced that he had supplied 4,000 rifles, 2,000 revolvers, 6 machine guns and ammunition to the Free State Government. When questioned on this in the House of Commons he replied that the Free Staters under the terms of the Treaty were free to buy arms anywhere in the world and might just as well get them from His Majesty's Government. Collins however gave the British rifles, which would have been embarrassing if identified being used against their suppliers, to the Cork Division and got back from Cork an equivalent number to use in attacks on the North.

No. 2 Division H.Q. was about ten miles from Maghera in the Six Towns; Battalion H.Q.'s were at a Glen a mile from Maghera. Ballymacpeake near

Innisrush and Magherafelt. The total I.R.A. strength in the Six Counties rose to about 8,500 men.

Soon after the Treaty fierce rioting in Belfast and shooting along the Border became daily events. Many men were killed and two complete families, one loyalist, one nationalist, were wiped out with their children. March, April and May 1922 were the stormiest months in the history of the Province.

In Maghera ' B ' Special strength during this time rose to over five hundred men. Sergt. Charlie McFadden, an Upperlands man who had fought all through the war was shot in an ambush at Claudy. On Sunday 19th March the I.R.A. Regulars struck heavily from the Sperrin Mountains. Most ' B ' men in the District had been mobilized for the day, stopping and searching cars, but were dismissed at 8 p.m. George McDonald, H/C. of Tobermore, had told the D.C. he expected an attack on the nearby Moyola Bridge and was keeping a close watch on it. At 6.30 that evening an Evangelist meeting was held in Tobermore with a famous speaker and many people went from all over the District to hear him. Special Constables Sandy Kirkpatrick and Jim Millar crossed the Moyola Bridge to go to Tobermore in plain clothes at a little after 8 p.m. without observing anything unusual. On their return an hour or so later, they were challenged at the approach to the bridge.

It was a very dark night and Jim Millar (who is still serving in the District) was searched and his Constabulary Identity Card removed, then he was marched forward to the Maghera side of the bridge. Many men were working at it with picks and shovels, their faces blacked. Another 'B' man, Bradley by name, also approached the bridge and was put under arrest; S/C. Joe Phillips arriving at the same time was warned to go home and say nothing. Jim Millar heard a shot but did not know what it meant. Some time later when the mining was complete, an I.R.A. officer gave the order, "Prisoners to Tobermore, I.R.A. men retire." Millar and Bradley were scarcely away from the bridge when it went up. The bombs said to have been constructed by a local blacksmith were made with explosives packed into the hubs of cartwheels. They only partly severed the bridge, but the explosion was heavy enough to rattle the plates on the dressers in Tobermore. Four unexploded bombs were found in the structure afterwards. Sandy Kirkpatrick was found shot through the heart from the front lying still astride his bicycle. It is possible that he had made an effort to get back to Tobermore to give warning and had been shot in the attempt or that he had at first mistaken the I.R.A. for a party of U.S.C. so bicycled on replying, "All right, I'm a 'B' man the same as yourselves," whereupon they shot him.

Meanwhile S/C. Joe Phillips had bravely crossed the river on stilts (which were in use at every riverside farm in those days) and arrived in Tobermore to give warning about fifteen minutes before the explosion. He was later commended for gallantry for this action. Only twenty rifles were available in the village at that time and to make matters worse George McDonald arrived without the keys for the box containing fourteen of these. He was said to have been approaching the bridge with six men when the explosion went off.

There are various accounts of what went on that night but it is certain at least that McDonald received very heavy criticism for the fact that the bridge was unguarded and his slow action in general. There was no follow up of the retreating I.R.A.

S/C. Joe Burns with several other Maghera ' B ' men had got across the bridge before the explosion but on arrival in Maghera they were arrested and held prisoner in old wallsteads in Hall Street. The I.R.A. had captured the barrack there the same night without firing a single shot, for a constable had betrayed the private signal which the patrol gave when they wanted to be let in. As soon as the door was opened the gunmen rushed in and locked the inmates in one of the cells. Their captures included 11 Service Rifles, 23 Revolvers, a Tommy Gun, 46 Mills Bombs and great quantities of ammunition as well as uniforms and record books.

The Moyola Bridge had been blown partly as a covering operation to delay the arrival of the Magherafelt platoon in case of a prolonged fight in Maghera. All telephones had also been cut and other roads blocked. But surprise was so complete that the I.R.A., ably commanded by Dan Donald, had retired before anyone in Maghera realized what had happened. They captured and took with them R.I.C. Sergt. MacKenzie, who they met off duty returning from visiting his future wife at Glen. He was forced to march fast with the retreating column but, when some of the men wanted to kick him on, Dan Donald stopped them. After two nights of hiding with his captors in the Sperrins, he was taken to Drumboe Castle, the Free

THE NORTH FIGHTS ON

State Army headquarters in Donegal. He was later held in various parts of that county and not released until five months had elapsed and a special application during an exchange of prisoners had been made by Sir James Craig. He had a remarkable knowledge of the face and habits of every man in the area and perhaps this was why he was removed; but the night after his disappearance a note was received by three leading Sinn Feiners in the area telling them that they could say their prayers if he was harmed. Sergt. MacKenzie who still lives in Portstewart had a colourful tale to tell on his return of the disorder in the enemy ranks. At times men were on hunger strike to protest at not being allowed to resign from the I.R.A. At others the Regulars kept the Irregulars prisoner or released them to help attack the British Forces, many of whom still remained south of the border.

Next day young Harry Clark the Adjutant delivered a further batch of rifles to Tobermore and had to go round by Curran as the bridge was impassable. His father had it repaired a few days later with trees cut from the plantation then very thick around Fortwilliam. Some twenty Fenians from the mountain were rounded up by No. 14 Platoon, Magherafelt, and forced to act as labourers for the job while Bob McClintock, the Upperlands works engineer supervised.

Four days after the blowing of the bridge, George McDonald's Flax Mill outside Tobermore was burned down. As a result the authorities were persuaded to post a platoon of 'A' men in Maghera and to mobilize 'B' men for duty in Tobermore, also in Upperlands to protect the works which after the burning of Flax Mills was considered a certain target.

Dr. Marshall commanded the mobilized men in Maghera until the arrival of a regular platoon. They were billeted in Victoria House (now the Post Office) to assist the R.U.C. and guard Largantogher the house of Colonel Clark H.M.L. which stood where the secondary school is today and was considered to be another certainty for attack since Shane's Castle near Antrim had been burned down very shortly before. The Maghera Platoon, No. 42, was first commanded by a Captain Truran. Truran refused to co-operate with the 'B's' whom he affected to despise and they twice fired on his Lancias when by his orders they refused to stop. To account for a shortage of ammunition in May he reported an ambush in The Sixtowns which never took place and he was shortly afterwards discharged.

After this the platoon was commanded by Lieut. Barr, one of the finest Platoon Officers in the County. He had been second in command in Magherafelt, and now co-operated very closely with Dr. Marshall. They were handicapped by the close watch kept on their movements; every time a Lancia left Maghera a window was lighted in the upper part of the town where it could be seen over the whole Brae Face.

In Tobermore the Orange Hall became the barrack. Seventeen men were mobilized and sandbagged positions set up in the centre of the village and at Killytoney cross-roads a mile down the Desertmartin Road. George McDonald at first was in charge but on 15th

April he died suddenly of a heart attack after a heated argument in the Hall. Captain C. L. G. Wilkinson then took charge for a short period, to be succeeded after his departure to England by Captain B. M. Padmore, an acquaintance of Mr. H. Wilkinson J.P., who also took a keen interest in the running of the Specials although he never appears to have an official position in the Force. He used to pay privately two ' B ' men to guard his house at night. " Black " Davy Nelson, who was a member of the Platoon, recalls Padmore as very active and completely fearless. He had a narrow escape on 26th May, when smoking a cigarette outside the barrack. A bullet thumped into a sandbag about a foot from his head; Sergt. Willie Hassan played a leading part in beating off the attack. After this steel shutters were fitted to the barrack windows. Under Padmore the Tobermore post became most efficiently organised but he was afterwards criticised for expenditure on what would appear to be entirely necessary items such as torches and alarm clocks for the men serving. Money was a constant worry to those trying to administer the force. With the rapidly increasing strength, frequent change in personnel and untrained administrative staff it was almost impossible to keep accounts for pay and equipment up to date.

Padmore was later transferred to take charge of Arms Permits in Derry and Sergt. Craig took over in Tobermore. The platoon there was in existence for about six months in all.

The Upperlands mobilized men were billeted in part of the Lapping Room of Wm. Clark & Sons, overlooking the Hall Field, in what is now the fireproof book safe. Sergt. John Burke was sent over from Headquarters in Derry to take charge and on 27th March, he tells how after arrival by train he walked up to Ardtara to report. The maid told him the family were at dinner but he could overhear the comments as she gave his message, "Burke?" "Can't be Sergt. Burke; he was shot in Swatragh last year!" A few minutes later a tall lean figure came out with his hands clasped behind his back; it was old Harry Clark, suspecting an impostor. After a few minutes conversation had established the visitor's bona fides, he brought his hands out to reveal a revolver: a moment later out came another six footer, Tom Clark, carrying his hat in his hand—this also concealing a revolver, to be followed by his younger brother Harry, just as tall and with a revolver and an automatic stuck in his belt!

Bunks were quickly built in the Post and blankets and equipment came from Derry, including bombs and handcuffs. Two men were put on guard at the works each night, while other patrols moved round the Gipsy Walk and the dams. A standing lookout was maintained on top of the hill behind Ardtara; this gave an exceptionally good all round view and a bearing table was constructed with marks and sighting arms so that the precise position of any fire, flare or light could be very quickly determined. The works horn was an alarm signal and frequently foiled I.R.A. attempts.

Patrols used to go out at 10 p.m. and return at about 4 a.m. In spite of the seriousness of the situation there was no ration allowance for food on these occasions and the men had to provide their own. Harry Clark and his brother Alex of Ampertaine used to take in turn to provide milk and food every night for the Upperlands patrol, but the men on their return found that all the milk that was left over had been drunk. One night Dan Scott and Dempsey of Tamlaght planned to find " The Cat " that was drinking it. So they got some special " jellup " from the chemist in Maghera and put it in the milk. When they came back one of the sergeants was sitting in the lavatory and complained that he had been there for about two hours. After that they lost no more milk!

Another evening a parade of the entire Upperlands post for inspection and arms drill was held; S/C. Tommy Lamont was a little late in arriving and one of the other men kindly offered to pack his haversack for him. It seemed a bit heavy but Tommy had no time to investigate, so slung it over his shoulder and fell in. After they had been marching for most of an hour, Sergt. Burke told Tommy he wasn't holding himself straight. " Why can't you get your shoulders back like the others?" he yelled. " Jesus, Sergeant, I'm strangled," said Tommy, making an effort to do so and it was not until afterwards he discovered a large stone had been inserted into his pack!

There was a good deal of skylarking of this sort and Dan Scott remembers Adams, the works carter, laughing so hard at the horseplay in the barrack that he put his jaw out of joint and had to go off to the doctor with it jammed open!

At first the mobilized men had only caps, bandoliers,

armbands and rifles, but by August they were equipped with full uniform and great coats, much of it old R.I.C stuff. The parsimonious British Government had sold this off and the 'B' men had to buy it back from such firms as Milletts out of their own pockets. Harry Clark, the District Adjutant in May sent off a cheque for over £100 for goods of this sort, having to instruct that they be sent in several separate parcels to reduce the risk of them being stolen by " Shinners " en route.

The accommodation too was gradually improved; an additional room and defences being specially built, until by June 1922 an Inspecting Officer, Colonel Dobbs, described it as one of the strongest posts in Ulster.

Chapter 5

THE CRISIS OF THE BATTLE

*We know when all is said
We perish if we yield.*
          From " Ulster " by Kipling

RECORDS of local events in 1922 are far from complete. Many of the deeds done are in any case best forgotten, but a district letter file running from March to July that year has luckily been preserved. On 30th March, Harry Clark wrote as follows to his neighbouring D.C.s.

Norman Stronge Esq., Aghadowey.
Warren Mann Esq., Bellaghy.
Hugh Thompson Esq., Coagh.

I have been discussing the whole situation with Dr. Marshall and some friends, and we all agree that unless we are better supported by the authorities it will be impossible for the ' B ' Force to protect the lives and properties of the loyalists in South Derry.

I need not remind you of what has happened during the past two weeks, murders and outrages of every description, which if unpunished are certain to be repeated.

I know that at present we are getting blame for not having prevented these outrages, and I feel that the few hundred ' B ' men even if mobilized all the time could not possibly guard all the points of danger throughout the County, the enemy having the advantage of being able to concentrate on any given position.

We are all strongly of the opinion that it is absolutely essential for the authorities to arrange for a big comb out of the enemy strongholds with full power at least to intern all the leaders.

I feel that we must consider our own position. It is very likely that if things remain quiet for a month or two the Platoon in Maghera will be withdrawn, then the Sinn Feiners will have a free field to come down and massacre us all. We will all be marked men, and our positions certainly serious and dangerous.

So far no offensive movement has been made against the three or four hundred men who marched into Maghera and cleared out the Police Barrack, murdered Kirkpatrick, blew up the Moyola Bridge, captured Sergt. MacKenzie, and burned down George McDonald's Mills. Flushed with these great victories they will now feel strong enough for further outrages, and I feel that the position is dangerous and urgent.

My idea is that we should all have a meeting and send in an ultimatum to the Prime Minister threatening resignation unless active measures are taken at once. At present we are only making ourselves marked men, and no object can be achieved as long as we are confined to our present strictly defensive measures.

Could you make it convenient to come here for a conference on Monday next, 3rd April, at 4 p.m.

Yours sincerely,

Harry Clark

The next morning news of another truce was in the papers. Michael Collins, who was frequently in London on his Government's business had there met

THE CRISIS OF THE BATTLE

Sir James Craig and concluded an agreement known as the Craig/Collins Pact.

This was hard to reconcile with Collins' recent activities in supporting attacks on the North. Those organised from his Headquarters at Beggars Bush near Dublin were to cease but he was in no position to enforce his wishes on the Irregulars, several units having declared themselves "anti-treaty" at an Army Convention only four days earlier. Rioting in Belfast had been particularly severe, and Collins felt that the Sinn Feiners there were getting the worst of it. The Pact provided for the lifting of the I.R.A. boycott on goods from Belfast, while Craig undertook to take special measures to see that the Nationalist minority in the North were given fair play. The British Government took a benevolent interest in the arrangement.

Harry Clark's letter to the County Commandant two days later must reflect the feeling of most loyalists in the North on receipt of the news.

On 4th April he wrote as follows referring to the Pact and to a threatening letter (quoted below) which he had received.

The County Commandant,
LONDONDERRY.

My dear Colonel,

I attended Craig's Meeting in Belfast yesterday, they are going to raise £100,000 for propaganda at once.

I am afraid from all I can hear that the peace terms are not worth the paper they are written on. I received a letter as enclosed copy on Friday night last, which is also in my opinion not worth the paper it is written on, and does not cost me a thought; unfortunately, however, Mrs. Clark, saw it and of course is more or less anxious. Sir Hiram Wilkinson got two, one a duplicate of mine, and the other said that if he or anyone assisted to repair the Tobermore Bridge they would be shot, as the destruction of this bridge was an act of war by the I.R.A. Now I don't know how this strikes you, but it has at least given a record in writing that the I.R.A. are at war with us, and why in Hell should we be at peace with them. Personally as you know, it has only been due to my very special efforts that peace has been kept in this district and that our men have not retaliated for the brutal murders of Kirkpatrick and McFadden. So far as I know there has not been a single act of retaliation in my area, but if there is another murder although I have no connection with it, I understand a body has been formed who will immediately destroy hundreds of Roman Catholics. About this there is no possible doubt.

Did you see that Mrs. McFadden got £3,000 for the loss of her husband? This is very satisfactory.

The Sergeant is having trouble with the 'A' men here who say they cannot stick out to the work guarding all the mills and private houses every night. We are losing Clark today, and would require seven more mobilized 'B' men immediately, which I hope you will allow me to mobilize, in fact I think you already told me I might take on as many men as I thought necessary. Craig said yesterday that Winston Churchill had promised him any amount of money he required, and it would be cheaper to take a few men to guard our property than to lose a quarter of a million if it is burned out.

This was the threatening letter which he enclosed: a curious mixture of polish and bad grammar.

OGLAIGH Na h-Eireann.

To
H. J. Clark, Esq.,
Ardtara, Upperlands.

Sir,

The brutal murders committed by the political party to which you belong upon Catholics in Belfast and North East Ulster generally have appalled civilisation. This vendetta of murder torture and cruelty has passed the limit of human endurance and no matter how much we dislike the methods employed by your people we are forced at least for the present to adopt them. The most dense can plainly see that it is useless in observing Christian principles when dealing with such a savage tribe.

Therefore we warn you that if this murder campaign does not stop immediately, and if any of our people in these Northern Counties come to further harm you will be one of the men in this area held directly responsible and you may consider your life forfeited and your property confiscated.

BY ORDER, I.R.A.

During the next few days while it appeared that the Pact might work, I.R.A. strangers openly visited a public house in the upper end of Maghera. They were recalled at night by their own military police, and it was evident that an I.R.A. force was present in the Brae Face. Two days afterwards, S/Sergt. R. Smith went to this pub for a drink, and foolishly took his rifle with him. He was met by some of these I.R.A. warriors, shot and severely wounded, and his rifle captured. This situation demanded action of some sort. Dr. Marshall arranged a rifle shooting practice for his Platoon at Kirley, the region of the Brae Face most likely to be the I.R.A. Headquarters. The practice would provide an opportunity of reconnaisance and might yield information. Lieut. Barr of the 'A' Platoon co-operated and the men were taken up in batches to Kirley in the Lancia, the returning Lancia taking home those who had fired their course.

On the way up a notice was seen on a tree at the entrance to a disused farmhouse. It read, "I.R.A. Keep Out." This was evidently their H.Q. Rifle practice further up the hill was proceeded with but when the last batch had almost finished they came under fire from a distance, some of the bullets arriving uncomfortably close. In rough country, with turf-banks and whin hedges, it was difficult to spot the source, and first Lieut. Barr and then Dr. Marshall ran across an open field to draw the enemy fire and locate their position, during which process a bullet lit at the heel of Dr. Marshall's boot. Finding it impossible to detect their position, and as the party was now small in number and ammunition nearly finished, it was agreed to retreat to the Lancia and wait further down the road. On the way down Lt. Barr and Dr. Marshall decided to pay a call at the I.R.A. H.Q. and enquire what they meant by breaking the Truce. Accordingly

THE CRISIS OF THE BATTLE

they took off their revolvers and unarmed went up to the door. Getting no response to their knocking, in the jargon of the Police Court they "effected an entrance." They found in the "Barrack Room" rows of neatly made camp beds and cooking equipment, but the house was otherwise unoccupied. Dr. Marshall picked up a small group photograph which Intelligence subsequently declared to be that of a Flying Column from Cork or Kerry.

A plan was then made to take a small party up to Kirley that night and bomb the I.R.A. out. But after a long stealthy approach it was found on arrival that the birds had flown. Next day they were reported to be harbouring in an empty house further north and it too was visited by a bombing party, but the Column had gone again and were seen no more in the area.

Rioting soon broke out in Belfast again and Michael Collins realizing that he could not in any case prevent attacks on the north made this the excuse for abandoning any undertakings he had made in the Pact. It had proved completely useless. The Northern Divisions of the I.R.A. began to co-ordinate for a great attack about the middle of May. First they wanted to carry out a plan to capture a Belfast Police barrack by a ruse and with it some armoured cars.

Following the threatening letter an attempt was made one night to burn Ardtara and shoot the Clark household. This was forestalled by S/Sergt. John McClean, then the gardener (grandfather of Alex who joined in 1956). McClean saw some movement when going to stoke the boilers, woke the household and the attackers were driven off. In the morning their footprints could be seen clearly.

The I.R.A. were confident of success, and even drew lots for who would get the big houses when victory was won! Harry Clark found out who had drawn Ardtara and sent him a note asking if he would kindly let him have a wee room at the back "for himself and the Missus." But there was little time for joking. In the last week in April, twelve murders took place in Belfast alone.

Things continued to get worse instead of better. On 28th April Harry Clark in writing to Lieut. Munn of No. 14 Platoon remarked *"Matters seem to have taken a very serious turn during the last few days and I am afraid the crisis is not far off."* He was dead right.

On 2nd May Sergt. Burke visiting the lookout patrol at the hilltop saw flares to the east. "That's Bellaghy," he guessed and trained the sighting arm on the bearing table. A flash of a torch at the markings confirmed that he was correct. He called Mr. Harry who promptly fired three shots, the signal to the works watchman to sound the horn and turn out the whole place. When an Upperlands patrol reached Bellaghy they found Constable Harvey dead, but the Barrack safe. A farewell party had been taking place for one of the Constables and a Bellaghy 'B' man was spending the evening in the Barrack. Constable Harvey went out into the yard and just after he had returned, the door (which should have been locked) suddenly opened and a masked I.R.A. Tommy Gunner and three companions stepped into the hall. One entered the day room but the 'B' man was left standing behind the opened door and managed to shoot the I.R.A. leader through the woodwork and get the outer door closed. He was ably assisted by Constable Stanage, the Barrack orderly. The light went out and Constable Harvey was shot during the scuffle. Sergt. Kerr and Constables Ross and Forde were all wounded. A follow-up party of the 'B's' made some contact with the enemy, and three were captured. In addition a few days later there was a new grave in the nearby Church Island graveyard. Another volunteer had "gone to Ameriky."

The same night at about midnight, a lorry load of men drew up outside Draperstown Barrack (which was then on the Desertmartin Road, not the present building) and asked for admission, saying they were the Platoon from Magherafelt. Sergeant Kiernan was suspicious. "Who is your officer?" "Barr," was the reply. "What are his initials?" The answer to this was a burst of machine gun fire through the door and the attack started.

It lasted more than two hours, the Sergeant and a Constable being wounded, but the Barrack saved. Hugh Lyle a 'B' man from Mormeal and a great loyalist was there as well that night, having brought in news of road blocks at Altigoan Bridge and on the Tobermore Road, which put the Barrack on the alert.

The next night three policemen left Ballyronan Barrack at about 10 p.m. on patrol. It was a clear but cold summer evening and several men in trench coats overtook them, one saying, "It's a sharp night."

"It is, boys," said Sergeant Frizelle, and with that the overtakers drew pistols and shot the policemen down. One Hegarty, was killed on the spot. The Sergeant and the other policeman, shot through the stomach, died in great agony a few hours later.

Two police squads coming to the support of the barrack were ambushed, one at Toome, the other by a strong party with a searchlight at Castledawson. The police had to abandon the car and continue the fight from the fields. The same night a 'B' man was shot dead in another ambush near Cookstown. The bridge at Ardnullagh by Swatragh was blown up for the second time.

There was another attack on Bellaghy as well, this time an attempt to burn Ballyscullion House. The gunmen were kept back for some time by old Mrs. Bruce, aged 75, who moved from window to window, clad only in her nightie with three shotguns and two loaders and kept up a steady barrage of fire! The army were at Ardtara that night and just in from a long patrol round Glenshane when the reports of shooting reached the house, so they at once set out again. Willie Clark drove the Rolls-Royce Armoured Car as a mist had come down and the army driver was very short-sighted. Unfortunately they clashed on arrival with one of the 'A' Platoons, both sides mistook the other for enemy and in the exchange of fire a man was wounded in the leg, but the men with tins of petrol crouching in the trees beside Ballyscullion gave it up and made off.

A letter appearing in the *Belfast Newsletter* on 6th May, gives an insight into the sort of thing which occurred nightly and what people were feeling.

"MURDEROUS ATTACKS ON POLICE BARRACKS IN DERRY."

"*On Tuesday night last I viewed the whole situation from midnight until 4 a.m. from a high hilltop, and it reminded me of what one was accustomed to see during the Great War in France. Signals were being exchanged by the Sinn Feiners all along the Sperrins with their friends who were murdering the police in Bellaghy, etc. Verey lights were going up from the barracks that were being attacked, and the same game was being played by the Sinn Feiners to try to draw the Crossleys in the wrong direction.*"

"*Is the Government going to protect us and relieve the danger?*"

"*If the answer is 'No' the people here will defend themselves.*"

(Signed.) "*One who thinks we have taken enough lying down.*"

The same week a Maghera 'B' man arrived in great excitement at Dr. Marshall's house about ten o'clock one night, reporting that he had seen large numbers of men trenching the road near Dreenan. The Doctor and Lieut. Barr were at first sceptical and suggested that his eyes were multiplying but he stuck to the story until the conversation was interrupted by the sound of firing from the north east. The officers were unable to decide if this came from Bellaghy or Portglenone so split the platoon and sent one party in each direction. The Crossleys travelled at top speed as usual but the 'B' man pursuaded them to heed his warning as they approached Dreenan. They slowed down and so were just able to pull up when the driver observed a dark patch on the road. It had been trenched up for a distance of some thirty feet. The soil had all been carefully removed and placed in the fields at either side, so without the warning many of the occupants of the front vehicle would have been injured. This cut proved a greater inconvenience to the local Nationalists than to our own forces so was left for some time but later repaired with the unwilling assistance of a squad of local men. The 'B' man was subsequently given a Favourable Record and a sum of money for his information.

The crisis was indeed not far off, but the new Ulster Government acted just in time, prompted at last by the increase in the reprisals which moderate men so greatly feared. On 12th May, three brothers called McKeown were taken from their beds and shot in cold blood at Ballymulderg near Magherafelt. There were similar incidents in many other parts. On 19th May after the Hiring Fair in Desertmartin, Starrett's Flax Mill was burned to the ground. The walls still stand there today four storeys high as a grim reminder of the night that followed. Three other mills had recently been burned locally as well as an attempt made on one in Culnady; there had been burnings in Limavady and Portglenone. The temper of the loyalists of Desertmartin was at boiling point, for the murders of the Ballyronan policemen had roused the fury of the whole countryside. Later that night in Desertmartin a pub, an egg store and three or four houses were burned. Four men were taken from their beds and shot a short distance from the village. The spot where their bodies were found is still pointed out, a hollow on the west side of the road through Durnascullion near where it joins the Desertmartin—Cullion Road. Up until recently it was always bare of grass, some maintaining that this was because nothing would grow where innocent blood had been spilt, others that the results were achieved by judicious use of paraffin.

Young Harry Clark was on patrol in Upperlands that night with Sergt. John McClean's section. Desertmartin was strictly speaking out of his area but he drove at high speed in the direction of the fires and shooting. A front wheel came off the Marmon near Grillagh Crossroads and held them up for a while. On arrival in Desertmartin it was impossible to drive up the street for the smoke, crowds and piles of furniture from the houses which had been burned.

The volume of similar incidents in other parts of the country may be gauged from the fact that the sack of Desertmartin and four men's deaths only rated nine inches of a single column in the Belfast papers.

A fifth man was killed five weeks later when he returned from the south and boasted in a pub that he was frightened of no one. He was taken from his house the same night after a long fight and later found shot on the railway line. After this for many months the men of many families near Desertmartin slept out " in the moss " or in the fields at night rather than risk being found in their beds.

The terrible truth, almost unbelievable today, is that such vendetta shootings were a commonplace in that grim period. Anyone who doubts this has only to look up newspapers of the day and see the awful record. Only by the influence of such men as Harry Clark and Dr. Marshall were murders prevented in the Maghera District.

The I.R.A. attempt to capture a Belfast barrack timed for the same week luckily failed and their grand attack was postponed.

At last the Government acted. On 24th May the I.R.A. and several of its brother organisations were declared illegal. " Rounding up the Rebels," " Six County Sweep," read the newspaper headlines next morning. Almost five hundred Sinn Feiners were arrested within twenty four hours of the proclamation, most taken unawares and without resistance. A wooden hulk the " Argenta " was converted into a prison ship and moored in Belfast Lough to accommodate them. The arrests included a number of professional men. Round Maghera the platoons helped by ' B's ' arrested several men. In Garvagh the papers relate that a school teacher named Murphy was shot and wounded while attempting to avoid arrest.

Many who evaded arrest went " on the run." The National Army or Regulars arranged courses of instruction at the Curragh Camp for such men from the North and their absence further weakened the I.R.A. in the field.

This period saw the gradual disbanding of the Royal Irish Constabulary which had been founded in 1836 and granted the prefix Royal for conspicuous bravery and loyalty displayed in the suppression of the Fenian Rising in 1867. The R.I.C. is widely acknowledged to have been one of the finest police forces ever known and it is a source of pride to the Specials that they were associated for their first months of existence with such great-hearted men.

The Royal Ulster Constabulary were being formed, many recruits coming from the disbanding R.I.C., others from the Specials. The Specials were at first renamed the " Royal Ulster Special Constabulary " but were not eventually authorised to retain the prefix. Colonel Wickham became the first Inspector General, a position he was to hold until 1946. The original idea and the shape of these forces owed much to a great Ulster Field Marshal, Sir Henry Wilson, one of Britain's war leaders. He had retired as Chief of the Imperial General Staff only two months earlier and now represented N. Down at Westminster. He had a poor opinion of all politicians and as anarchy continued in the South and the Provisional Government seemed unable to cope, he called on 21st May in Parliament for Britain to reimpose Union on the whole island! Public opinion there was however still far from favourable to Ulster and could rapidly have turned to open hostility. Reports of reprisals against Nationalists did immense damage as they were usually exaggerated in the Press. It was the constant worry of those in command to stop acts of vengeance taking place.

The following notice circulated round the Maghera District illustrates the problems:

Upperlands,
25th May, 1922.

NOTICE TO "B" MEN

I am glad to say that with a few exceptions all the 'B' men in my unit, No. 3 Area have been congratulated on three occasions by the G.O.C. on the splendid discipline they have maintained often in the face of great provocation. This discipline is very helpful to the Prime Minister, as the other side are always trying to get a chance of blackening the Specials, and in England they are only too ready to listen to such reports and to cry us down. You must know how very important it is for us to keep the English people with us, they could withdraw the Army any day and leave us to the tender mercies of 100,000 Shinners from the South and West, so I urge all of you to continue the good behaviour that has been in this area, and do not give any unnecessary provocation.

I will not tolerate any drinking or unlawful behaviour of any description.

Signed: H. J. Clark
District Commandant No. 3 Area.

On June 22nd the English public had their eyes rudely opened when Field Marshal Wilson was shot dead outside his London house probably by orders from Collins. Both the gunmen concerned were caught and later executed. Still the British Government wavered. To meet the threat of them withdrawing the Army (then about 13 battalions strong in Ulster) the 'C.I.' Division was formed of some 20,000 Special Constables organised to move and fight as an army unit. Based in Belfast they trained like the Territorial

Army, had their own transport and became highly efficient.

The Great Round-up on 24th May was followed by the imposition on 1st June of a Curfew over the whole country. Penalty for being out after 11 p.m. was £10 fine or a month in jail. This was rigidly enforced. Anyone caught unless well known, was liable to get a hammering from the 'A' men or the Army as well as being brought up in court. The Norfolk Regiment shot a man dead near Magherafelt when he ran away after being challenged. On the second night of the Curfew, Moneymore District "arrested" Sir Dawson Bates, the Minister of Home Affairs, accompanied by Major Gunning, their D.C., and were congratulated on their alertness.

One night several Tamlaght men were on patrol in the village when they heard footsteps and spied someone approaching. It was a wee old mountainy man. "Ma wee horse is dead," he explained, "I'm going to Ballymena to buy a powny." "Have you any pistols on you?" they asked jocularly. "Nothing," said he, "except £30 for the powny." The patrol agreed among themselves to let him go on but cautioned him to tell no one that they had stopped him. Fortunately, two or three of the 'B' men afterwards decided to see him safely on his way, for a mile or so down the road they arrived in the nick of time to prevent another party, possibly having overhead the conversation, posing as 'B' men and robbing him of the money.

At the height of the trouble, the District Clerk, Ernie Lee, managed to find time to get married. This was on the 24th May. A few weeks later he and his wife had a rude shock when some shots were fired through the roof of their house. Percy and George Clark who were on patrol nearby at the "road engines" that night heard the shooting and thinking that a big attack was in progress immediately dashed off to warn Sergt. Burke and the Platoon. Much later it was established that a 'B' man with drink taken had fired the shots. The next day H. F. Clark went with the Sergeant from Maghera to disarm him. He fired a shot as they entered the house, which went into the wall about a foot above their heads, before giving in.

As well as the Curfew, sweeps by the army became more frequent. The Lancashire Regiment came from Derry, particularly at the weekends. Captains Wood and Rochier used to sleep at Ardtara and the men in the Ampertaine hayloft, which was used at other times as a drill hall for the 'Bs.'

Raids and patrols were generally accompanied or directed by Maghera District officers. On one of these sweeps S.D.C. Tom Clark was searching a farm house and poked his head up through a hatch to examine the loft; he was shaken to see a dead policeman lying there, and shouted to the men with him about this, but on examination they found it was simply a dummy dressed in captured uniform, perhaps to be used as a decoy for an ambush.

On another occasion after a search proved fruitless young Harry knocked over a kitchen table, and a rifle and bullets were found secured underneath it.

At the same time many roads were trenched or "cut" to channel traffic through points where they

Sir James Craig Inspecting Maghera District

Sir James Craig, Prime Minister of Northern Ireland, inspects the Maghera District in December, 1922. Mr. H. J. Clark walking to his left in plain clothes.

Portstewart Training Camp, 1923

As the inscription in the picture shows, the force at this time was known as the Royal Ulster Special Constabulary.

Officers at Portstewart Camp, 1923

Front Row — Capt. Barney Boyle, M.C., City Adjutant; Lieut. Munn, Camp Commandant, O.C. No. 14 Platoon, Magherafelt; Lieut.-Col. George Moore-Irvine, County Commandant; Capt. Austin, Ex-R.C.M.P., O.C. Dungiven Platoon; D.C. Wylie, Derry City.

Back Row — S.D.C. Frazer, Derry City; S.D.C. H. F. Clark, Adjutant, No. 3 District; Lieut. Gordon, Platoon Officer, Co. Derry; S.D.C. Kilgore, Derry City; S.D.C. Ritter, Limavady; Lieut. Barr, O.C. Maghera Platoon; S.D.C. Dr. R. L. Marshall, Maghera.

Smartness on parade

[Photo by courtesy "Northern Whig"

Upperlands team representing County Londonderry at Newtownards in 1933: Col. Sargent, D.S.O., M.B.E. (Staff Officer), S/C. George Morrow, S/C. R. Henry, S.D.C. H. F. Clark, S/C. Jim Clarke, S/C. R. Vallelly. Upperlands finished second in the Six Counties on this occasion.

THE CRISIS OF THE BATTLE

could be readily checked. The Mullagh Road, the Tivaconaway-Swatragh Road and the Ballinahone-Lisnamuck Road were a few treated in this way.

Early in June the I.R.A. made their only attempt at open invasion across the Border. Belleek and Pettigo were occupied but after consultation with Churchill the army counter-attacked in two battalion strength and quickly drove them out.

The Round-up, the Curfew, and the increased army activity were making things very difficult for the terrorists. At the same time, they began to get deeply involved in the Civil War in the South, which started full scale with the burning of the Four Courts in Dublin on 28th June.

Something like 500 officers and men of the 2nd and 3rd Northern I.R.A. Divisions took advantage of the training at the Curragh and this also had much to do with the cessation of " action " in the North. Many of those who went joined the Free Staters—Dan Donald McKenna was one of them—others joined the Irregulars. Of the Southern experts sent north several now went back and joined their Irregular comrades. Others were not so lucky. Charlie Daly, O.C. 1st Northern Division, and Sean Larkin of Bellagherty, Co Derry, were captured by their opponents in the Civil War and executed at Drumboe Castle, Co. Donegal in March, 1923.

How the Civil War would go none could tell, but by mid-summer, Ulster was relatively quiet.

Chapter 6

ULSTER GETS HER BREATH

*An' whin the Army faced about, 'twas just in time to find
A couple o' policemin had surrounded us behind.*
Percy French.

THE lull in the fighting was put to good use by the Specials in training and re-organisation. Renewed attacks, victory for the I.R.A. and the country being made too hot for loyalists to live in still seemed a very real possibility. " Give em the Lead " O'Duffy had said so at Armagh in September 1921.

Maghera District at this time was almost up to the full allowed numbers.*

' C ' Specials were however still being recruited in July, and the strength in this category of the District rose to a total of over 120. Firearms were now so strictly controlled that an outlying householder who wanted one for protection found that the best way of getting a permit was to join the ' C's.' The Army and platoons raided loyalist and Sinn Fein houses alike for arms. Amateur lady searchers were called to help the ' B's ' on occasions when they stopped a train or a bus. Some of these were said to have been remarkably thorough!

On 7th July, Commander Jim Clark R.N., Rtd., of Moyola Park, who had won a good D.S.O. at

---

* Made up as follows: Tamlaght 56, Culnady 44, Upperlands 125, Maghera 43, Tobermore 91. A total of 359, for which were held 322 weapons, 250 rifles and 72 revolvers.

Zeebrugge was appointed Area Commander in succession to Col. McCalmont. He re-organised things rapidly and in a series of Confidential Area Orders drew up plans for all eventualities. A general invasion in strength across the border—Operation M.Q. to concentrate 200 men and fifty cars quickly at any point —and Operation C.A.R. to cordon off selected areas were three of these. His bluff naval manner sometimes rubbed 'B' men up the wrong way but his methods produced results. Young Harry Clark, the Adjutant was given an appointment in command of a Platoon in the "Derry Borderers' a force prepared to meet a sudden emergency by doubling the number of mobilised platoons at a few hours notice. To raise standards of training a camp under canvas was set up at Portstewart. Each 'B' man was to attend for a fortnight and although this was not compulsory the response was excellent. Lieut. Munn acted as Camp Commandant and Col. Moore-Irvine visited the training most days. These camps gave a great chance for officers and men from all over the county to get to know each other, though sometimes feelings ran high between the City and the County and they had to be separated!

The site used was below the Strand Hotel where O'Hara Drive is today. County Antrim held similar camps at Portrush and Ballycastle.

During the autumn Killytoney and Ballinahone Sub-Districts were formed by men drawn from Tobermore.

There were still occasional burnings and a platoon had been stationed at Desertmartin since the trouble there in May. On 8th August the officer in charge,

Lieut. Cooper, was shot. It appeared to have been an accident while out rabbit shooting.

The Civil War in the South raged fiercely. In August the Irregulars were driven out of Cork. " It's a dam' good job to see those Shinners shooting each other," was many a 'B' man's comment. The same month the Free Staters suffered two reverses; Griffiths, one of the more moderate and far seeing men in the movement, died of a brain haemorrhage. Shortly afterwards the Irregulars succeeded where the British had failed, and shot General Michael Collins. He had become famous as the fighting leader of the I.R.A. but spent his last months suppressing his old comrades.

Things in Ulster remained on the surface curiously peaceful. Would the Southern Government, now that Collins and Griffiths were dead, honour the Treaty? Churchill was in constant negotiation with Dublin and on 28th August was assured that they would.

At this time the Irregulars evacuated Glenveagh Castle in County Donegal, where they had been living " like lords' bastards " for months. The deer fence was cut by these liberal-minded men and stags and hinds roamed the country raiding crops and gardens. They shot out the eyes of all the portraits except that of King William for which they reserved a special honour. It was placed on the floor and each man eased himself on it before he left!

On 2nd December, the District had its first ceremonial parade for inspection by no less a person than the Prime Minister, Sir James Craig. This took place on the hill above Ardtara, chosen as being easy to guard against surprise attack. The Area Commander

ULSTER GETS HER BREATH 77

led the March Past, wearing police tunic and breeches surmounted by his naval commander's "brass hat"! The route taken was up the old Cow Loaning, past the Ardtara motorhouse to a Saluting Base in the field. Afterwards Sir James stayed the night with Alex Clark at Ampertaine House, and retired rather early. A maid going into the room to check that everything was all right was surprised to hear the loud challenge, "Who's there?" and see a pistol levelled at her! In the morning Sir James walked round the garden, and raised a laugh by saying how nice it was to see one bridge in Ulster not blown up —the ornamental one across the pond!

The Curfew produced many social complications. Dances had to run from midnight to 6 a.m. at least, which taxed the enthusiasm of all but the most energetic and only a few privileged people were able to get the passes isued by the Area Commander. Old James Davidson, the Ampertaine yardman, was always accustomed to being about his work at all hours of the night with a hurricane lamp, and when challenged by one of the army sentries guarding the vehicles, walked on saying, " Houl' yer tongue, it's only me! " so after this they gave him peace.

The only inspection so far to have been held of the entire Ulster Special Constabulary was held at Lisburn by Lord Derby then Home Secretary on 7th April 1923. For the District this meant a very long day being transported by rail up the Derry Central Line, now long since closed.

S.D.C. Harry Clark shared the Officers' carriage with Captain Norman Stronge, the Aghadowey D.C. (now

Sir Norman Stronge, Bt., H.M.L., M.C., Speaker of the House of Commons) S.D.C. Tom Clark, Captain Munn, O.C. No. 14 Platoon, Magherafelt, and others. On reaching Lisburn, they marched some 2½ miles out the Hillsborough Road to a large sloping field, on the left of the road at Sprucefield for the parade. On the way back as the train passed Drumagarner, near Kilrea, several bullets were fired at it and some passed through the carriages but luckily no one was hit.

The country slowly returned to normal but it took many years to repair the broken bridges and communications and longer still before the public came to expect law and order as a matter of course. Threatening letters still flew around and young Harry Clark received a total of three at various times.

On 23rd May 1923 came the end of the Civil War in the South. De Valera admitted defeat and the I.R.A. were, temporarily at least, out of business.

In June 1923 things had become so peaceful that the Judge at the County Assizes, then held in Coleraine, was given a pair of white gloves indicating no crime during the preceding six months. In July the same year old Harry Clark received the M.B.E. for his services in command of the District. There must have been many more who were worthy of the same honour without having received it. In him and Dr. Marshall, the District had been led by two of the greatest Ulsterman of the time.

Later this year the 'A' Platoons began to be disbanded, much to the dislike of the men concerned. In many parts of the country they mutinied demanding a pension or bounty. The Magherafelt Platoon locked

Lieut. Munn in his room and put an armed man at the door with instructions to admit no one. Commander Clark boldly walked up to the sentry in face of the threat " to blow his head off" disarmed him and quelled the trouble. When the Upperlands platoon was disbanded Sergt. Burke returned to Derry where he later acted as Adjutant to the 2nd Battalion of the Derry City Ulster Home Guard and U.S.C. Adjutant and did not retire until long after the War.

David John McIntyre, ex-bombing Instructor of the 10th " Skins ' became Sergeant Instructor in Maghera.

The Portstewart training camps were repeated in 1923 and 1924 but not afterwards.

In the South many ex-I.R.A. men joined the Civic Guard which had replaced the R.I.C. and right decent chaps they became in their new guise!

Gulladuff Barracks was re-opened in 1930 under a particularly able young Sergeant Albert Kennedy, later to earn a knighthood as our present Inspector General! This barrack was finally closed in 1950, while Innisrush closed in 1937.

By 1930 political troubles were obscured by the economic depression. The ' A ' Specials and ' C's ' had been disbanded and Government money was so tight that the ' B's ' paraded only once a year for the annual pay of 5/-. The office of County Adjutant was abolished but Captain Munn remained on by private arrangement with the County Commndant. When Bob Rainey who had recently moved to Upperlands from County Antrim inquired about rejoining the ' B's,' Bob Johnston, the Head Constable, advised him not to bother for, " I think," he said, " the whole thing will soon be finished." Then Craig, now Lord Craigavon, "Jimmy Not an Inch," stepped in and said positively that as long as he was Prime Minister there would be a Special Constabulary.

Ceremonial occasions brought detachments from the Counties to Belfast several times during the following years. In 1930 for the Prince of Wales' visit, in 1935 for Sir Edward Carson's funeral and in 1937 the visit of King George VI and Queen Elizabeth which was the most memorable for the Maghera man. Colonel McCrory, D.S.O., County Commandant, commanded the Derry County detachment which was billetted overnight in the Methodist Buildings, College Gardens. After a very early breakfast they marched to Balmoral to line the Royal Route, and returned to the billet for lunch. Some admirer had managed to insert a stink bomb into the truck carrying the sandwiches and almost all were inedible. In the afternoon the detachment marched many miles and was allocated a position of honour close to the Royal Yacht some two miles below the Queen's Bridge.

On the return journey an effort was made by the I.R.A. to blow up the train with the Londonderry City men at Templepatrick Bridge but the bomb failed to detonate.

The Sub-districts in the County were re-grouped more than once during this period and Maghera became known as No. 2 'B' District.

In July 1938 Mr. H. J. Clark, M.B.E., D.L., resigned as District Commandant due to advancing years. The 'Bs' presented him with a Hardy Trout Rod which he greatly prized. His son H. F. Clark, " young Harry " who had received one of the four Coronation Medals which came to the County the year before, was appointed in his place.

A few days later took place the "Maghera Riots." On 11th July 1938 a crowd from the Draperstown area and the Brae Face, three or four hundred strong, attacked the Maghera Barrack, and attempted to remove the Orange decorations from the town. Mr. Joe Burns was at this time Platoon Sergeant in Maghera and turned out at the same time as Upperlands 'B' men under the new D.C. Passing motor cars were commandeered to convey the Upperlands men quickly to Maghera where they found the police, under Sergeant Sturdy, being very heavily pressed with several men injured.

The combined forces under D.I. Dobbin, Magherafelt, put the Shinners to flight and afterwards over a hundred bicycles were found lying about the hedgerows on the upper side of the town. The owners naturally never claimed these and they were sold for the benefit of those injured in the fighting.

I.R.A. casualties were as usual never officially admitted but a song composed at the time mentions:

> *Nine or ten lie in the Glen,*
> *Well sheltered from the breeze.*

D.C. H. F. Clark, S.D.C. T. J. Clark, P/Sergts. Jim Clarke, Joe Burns and A/Sergt. Bradley all received Certificates of Merit for good service on this night. D.I. Dobbin, ex-R.I.C., later County Inspector, was a very good friend of the 'B' men. Road patrols were started at night once again and continued up until the beginning of the War. The I.R.A. at this time commenced a series of attacks on the public in general in England in which several people were killed.

On Wednesday 28th June 1939 the whole District paraded at Rockwood, Upperlands as guests of the District Commandant and his wife. The Salute was taken by the County Commandant then photos of each Sub-District were taken, also a general group, before the company got down to enjoying tea and Guinness.

It was on this occasion that one S.D.C. unfamiliar with ceremonial drill got his Platoon into forward motion for the March Past with the words " By the left, come on boys!"

The same year Nissen Huts were built at Upperlands and Tobermore, the first specially built accommodation ever provided.

Interest in shooting ran very high in the pre-war years and competitions were extremely keenly contested. Upperlands perhaps on account of their greater numerical strength were the best team on average, but in the .303 were beaten by Tamlaght in 1938 and 1939. The D.C. was a member of the teams which brought back the County Cup in 1930, 1933 and 1937 and only missed winning the Six Counties Final by the narrowest of margins. In the miniature competitions, Upperlands were unbeaten in the District for fifteen years between 1935 and 1950 but their undoing at County level was usually Aghagaskin, familiarly known as " The Boars!"

CHAPTER 7

A NEW ENEMY—1939/1945

*Stand up and take the War,
The Hun is at the Gate!*
                    Kipling.

ON the outbreak of war the U.S.C. re-commenced carrying out its basic function of road check points and continued with this duty for the duration, each man doing one four hour patrol per week. The D.C., S.D.C. T. J. Clark and many members of the District joined the Services, while others volunteered for mobilization with the R.U.C. Mr. Willie Clark, D.L., J.P. became D.C. As ever, England's difficulty was Ireland's opportunity. Just as in 1914 there were plenty of men in Southern Ireland with the incredible naivety to fancy that a free 32-County Ireland was a German War aim. This and blind hatred made them work for England's defeat.

I.R.A. wartime outrages were mainly confined to Belfast, but there was a constant risk of raids in any part of the country. There was undoubtedly some activity locally but it remained underground except for an occasional glimpse such as when a policeman on a tillage check in Slaghtneil happened to glance through the window of a derelict cottage to see a man bound to a chair and found that he had interrupted an I.R.A. court martial.

The blackout greatly increased the difficulties of

stopping cars at night and inevitably there were instances in every district where patrols had to open fire on vehicles which failed to halt. The first shot would be a warning one in the air the second or third in most cases got the back tyre. The fact that there were no cases in the District of anyone being killed or wounded is a tribute to the marksmanship and steadiness of the men who carried out these monotonous patrols usually after a hard day's work and in addition to Home Guard and firewatching duties.

The shooting was however not always successful. "It's a wonder that car didn't stop for I 'red' the rifle into her!" as one Tamlaght man related indignantly. He had crossed rifles of a marksman on his forearm so perhaps that car was manned by the I.R.A. Perhaps more likely by a drunk or a man out with somebody else's wife. One never knew.

The practice in those days was for one section to do duty each night split into two halves which walked the roads for four hours each in succession. The Upperlands platoon still used the Broghan House as headquarters and had tea there during the patrol. S.D.C. Jim Clark thought that at one time that some of the men were not washing up properly so he put up a notice to this effect and found next day that S/C. Willie Bradley (known as "The Poet") had added the following lines:

> *We are the gallant 'Bs,'*
> *Who bravely man the breeze,*
> *With us there is no bother*
> *We keep this place so neat and clean*

A NEW ENEMY

And shining like pure gold,
Us three sups and wash our cups
So mind the next patrol!

On another occasion P/Sergt. Crowe was trying out some new red cork insoles in his boots and found he had to cut off a bit to make them fit. Later when the sandwiches were being made up Tommy Dinsmore slipped a bit of the cork into one and saw it taken by Sammy Ballantyne who grew redder and redder as he tried to chew it. Still Sammy refused to give in while those in the know tried hard to control their faces. Eventually Tommy had to run outside and to burst out laughing so hard the tears ran down his cheeks! Another night one of the Sergeants remarked that he'd like a few scallions to add to the sandwiches. A Constable innocently said he knew a garden where a few could be raided so all the section had a great feed but in the morning the Sergeant found that it was his own garden which had been stripped bare!

On May 14th 1940 a fortnight before Dunkirk the Government called on able-bodied men throughout the U.K. to form Local Defence Volunteer units to repel the expected German invasion. Later Sir Winston Churchill renamed these the Home Guard. The Northern Ireland force retained the name L.D.V. long after the change had been made in England and was in many ways unique for the 'Bs' formed an invaluable nucleus of trained men at a time when the army urgently needed all its own instructors. Ulster Home Guard was the name finally adopted. Each U.S.C.

Sub-District recruited an equivalent number of men to form a second platoon of Home Guardsmen to be numbered in due course, with the others in the Company.* The 'Bs' at first wore their ordinary uniform with an U.H.G. Armband, and in the heat of the emergency no one worried much about the legal implications. Later it was realized that a policeman who opened fire on enemy forces was liable to be shot on capture under the Hague Convention. So the U.S.C. and H.G.'s newly issued black denims were replaced with khaki for H.G. duties, while the U.S.C. continued to patrol in police uniform at night; but it took the lawyers many months to sort out the tangle.

On 30th November 1940 in a speech at Lisburn, Lieut. General Sir Henry Pownall G.O.C. Northern Ireland District, paid tribute to the L.D.V.s and remarked that on account of the connection with the already trained U.S.C. they were far ahead of the English Home Guard.

Training was carried out on a scale and with an enthusiasm rarely seen in peacetime. Weekend training courses, field firing and all-night exercises came at frequent intervals. Road blocks of sandbags were set up and then moved at the whim of each new G.O.C. A Lewis Gun position was sited in Upperlands on the Lapping Room dam bank to defend the works from

* Mr. Willie Clark acted as 'A' (Maghera) Company Commander and Mr. C. G. L. Wilkinson commanded 'B' (Tobermore) Company. The Tobermore Company was originally commanded by Captain McKenzie, who came to the district at first as O.C. of the 'A' Special Platoon quartered at Derrynoid, Draperstown, in the 20's.

A NEW ENEMY

the air and an elaborate strongpoint built at Grillagh junction. By night the Home Guard manned observation posts and roadblocks and unlike the U.S.C. who still received their small but regular money did all for no pay.

At 0300 on 7th September, came the moment of truth. The invasion had started. . . . 'A' and 'B' Companies turned out to meet the Germans reported as advancing south after landing at Portrush. The Battle of Britain was at its height and the London Blitz just starting. This news seemed no more incredible than other daily realities of the time so many of those who left their wives and children in the early hours of a Sunday morning were convinced they were going to their last fight; they turned out nevertheless and manned slit trenches and weapon pits. . . . . . . but by breakfast time most of them were home. A section of Blackhill Platoon, 'B' Coy., reinforced the R.U.C. Barracks in Draperstown on this occasion. Nobody remembered they were there until long after everybody else had stood down, the section got in touch with H.Q. to find out how the invasion was going!

What appears to have happened is that the codeword "Cromwell" "Invasion Imminent," was issued to Army Commands in South East England to bring them from eight hours to immediate notice for battle and repeated for information only to outlying headquarters. An inexperienced staff officer somewhere in Northern Ireland assumed that action was required and rumour did the rest. "Cromwell" remained in force until 19th September, then the risk of the invasion began to recede.

Later Call-out plans became highly organized with platoon and section positions carefully preselected to meet attacks from various directions. Code letters and a secret transparent map overlay recorded the details. A big scale Company H.Q. map was laboriously constructed. On one exercise General Carton de Wiart V.C. ("one arm, one eye and one lung") visited the District and made a mild criticism of the site chosen for the Bren Gun. "If ye think ye can do any better," said the offended 'B' man, "just move her over yourself."

Another exercise near Upperlands became more exciting than the planners intended when the attackers ran out of blank ammo and proceeded to use live instead.

One evening an army football team was getting much the worse of it in a match in Upperlands when a 'B' man sidled up to the Army C.O. "Next time ye bring ones to kick agin us bring ones as can kick, for them can kick none," was his comforting advice.

Gas masks or respirators were carried on all exercises and one elderly Upperlands Home Guardsman got the right word by mistake when he referred to it at a kit inspection as his exasperator!

Lieut. Evan Burns, LL.D., M.A., M.B.E., recalls that the Rev. John Watson, Curate of Maghera, was a member of his Culnady platoon, and one day arrived on parade without the bolt for his rifle. These bolts were always stored in a separate place for security reasons and he had forgotten his. Sergt/I. McMillan wanted a rifle for demonstration purposes and happened to pick up that belonging to His Reverence. The

A NEW ENEMY 89

sergeant was only recently out of the army and like most of the people who join the 'Bs' from the forces had to go through a period of initiation before becoming used to their different ways. He produced a blistering string of oaths directed at the unknown owner of the rifle but even he was embarrassed when the Rev. John came forward to collect it.

As the Home Guard grew in skill and equipment, the higher organisation was changed to cover the vital defence line of the Bann. Maghera with the rest of the South Derry area as part of No. 3 Battalion, Co. Londonderry, under Colonel Nangle were brigaded with the County Antrim Battalions to form the Bann Valley Brigade under Captain Robby Hanson (Brigadier Hanson U.H.G.). The excellent scale of equipment eventually reached is indicated by the fact that the North Derry Battalion under Col. McCrory had by 1942, eight 25-Pounder field guns for the defence of the aerodromes. Some Platoons of the 3rd Battalion had sub-artillery Spigot Mortars. Others, like Blackhill Platoon, were specialists in Guerrilla warfare. There was a good deal of friendly rivalry between the 'A' and 'B' Companies, and some very good joint exercises were held. There was, for example the " Trojan Horse " attack on Maghera by 'B' Company. It was a most elaborate affair, involving a feint through Largantogher grounds carried out by the most approved methods of infiltration, and the real attack by the bulk of 'B' Company, who managed to drive straight into Maghera in lorries disguised as ordinary troops passing through. Rev. John Brown M.A., B.D., the 'B' Company Officer, now Lecturer in History at Magee College Londonderry, recalls; "It was well worth the trouble of having waded along the Mullagh burn (capturing and retaining the Largantogher butler for security reasons en route) and having died symbolically at the hands of the Maghera 'B' men and U.H.G. somewhere near the Presbyterian Church, to see the faces of the "high-ups" at the end of the exercise. For some reason no very particular task had been given to the Ballinahone 'B' men of 'B' Company, except to make a kind of demonstration towards Maghera. They had simply walked up the main road at their ease into Maghera R.U.C. Barracks, which was 'A' Company H.Q. and captured it! While everybody else was hotly engaged the Ballinahone men had achieved the whole object of the scheme, and were sitting with their feet up enjoying themselves!"

Courses in unarmed combat map reading, bombing and all forms of infantry work were held at the H.G. School in Ballynure under a particularly ferocious Training Officer, Captain Letchford.

In March, 1943 a Drill Competition typical of many others was held in the Upperlands Orange Hall for the Challenge Cup presented by Major C. B. McKenzie. Four teams took part—Maghera, Tobermore, Blackhill and Upperlands. Maghera* were declared the winners and Sergeant J. Lee was presented with the cup by Colonel Hanson who congratulated the team on their

---

*Blackhill under Sergeant Taylor were runners up. Those present included, Lt.-Col. Nangle R.E., Capt. C. G. K. Wilkinson, Capt. J. Burns, Lieut. George Clark, Lieut. J. A. C. Johnston, Lieut. R. E. Burns B.A., LL.B., 2nd Lieut's. J. A. Scott, Charles Clark and Ivan Clark, D. I. Stratford and Sergt. Brady R.U.C.

A NEW ENEMY

success and all the parade on their physical fitness and fine bearing.

One Sunday a live Mills Bomb practice was taking place in a bog near Upperlands; there was no proper throwing or priming bay the bombs simply being thrown over a turf bank. One Upperlands man threw his so badly that it hit the bank and fell back at his feet, whereapon all he did was lie down beside it and put his hand over his face. Mr. Willie Clark, with great agility and presence of mind stepped over him, picked up the grenade and got it over the bank a fraction of a second before it went off. Many people have been decorated for lesser acts.

By the time it stood down in January, 1944, the Home Guard had become a highly efficient force.*

It was reformed for a period in 1952 to meet the Russian threat but on this occasion remained quite separate from the U.S.C.

Towards the end of the war, re-forming the U.S.C. on its own and getting it back to its normal functions, as well as calling in and accounting for the great mass of U.H.G. equipment, was an immense task and we were lucky to have a very outstanding Adjutant at this period in Mr. George Evans, late South Irish Horse and Irish Fusiliers. He had succeeded Mr. Munn in 1943 and Captain Lenox-Conyngham of Moneymore had succeeded Col. McCrory as County Commandant and C.O. of No. 3 Battalion, U.H.G.

---

* The Officers of 'A' Company at this time were as follows: Lieut. Bob Barbour, P/Sergt. Sam Flynn, Upperlands; Lieut. H. Kyle, P/Sergt. J. A. Crockett, Tamlaght; Lieut. R. Evan Burns, P/Sergt. S. Graham, Culnady; and Lieut. Robert McCaughey, P/Sergt. R. Clark. Innisrush.

The future functions and status of the U.S.C. were still in considerable doubt when Mr. Willie Clark retired in August 1945, and handed the district back to Major H. F. Clark, on his return from the army. All ranks combined to give their retiring C.O. a particularly handsome presentation in the form of a revolving plinth with plates on each face one for each platoon engraved with the name of every man who had served in it. This was made by S/C. Tommy Arbuthnot, and designed and French polished by Pl/Sergt. Crowe. On the bottom was fastened one of the secret wartime call out maps.

The following story from Mr. Malcolm McKee, M.C., who was an original member of the U.V.F., might act as an epitaph on the war-time U.H.G. It was after Dunkirk and Mr. McKee, then in the Regular Army, was, like many others, curious as to the function of the force, and questioned a U.H.G. Sergeant who had been a Sergeant in the Inniskillings in the First War. "Tell me, Mr. Adair", he said, "what exactly are you supposed to do in the Home Guard? It has always been something of a mystery to me". "I don't quite know, Mr. McKee", said the Sergeant, "but so far as I can see, we are to hold the enemy while the Navy evacuates the Army".

It was a mystery no longer.

Chapter 8

SI PACEM VIS...

"IF you want peace, prepare for war" said the Romans two thousand years ago. The same maxim had to be Ulster's guide after 1945 for there was no indication that "VJ" Day meant any cessation of hostilities by the I.R.A.

The Specials carried on with road patrols for a while, but these were able to be discontinued soon and the force settled down to training and re-organisation.

Reports of the I.R.A. training, too, began to come in mainly in the form of weekend camps south of the Border. These went on over such a long period without any operational activity that one began to suspect that they partook more of a holiday than a military nature; but at the same time the I.R.A. were attempting to build a new more strictly disciplined organisation within the Province. During the war they had lost almost all their arms dumps around Belfast due to bad security. Now any of the men recruited were picked for their discretion and sobriety. Those with a criminal record or who had been interned during the war were not sought as recruits, and most local companies within the Province were believed to have an Intelligence Officer to check members' activities, as well as gathering information about the enemy. All were bound by a fearsome oath of loyalty to their comrades and the cause of achieving a 32-County Irish Republic by force.

Meanwhile, Col. Sargent D.S.O., M.B.E., who had been head of U.S.C. since its first beginnings and understood it as no other man could, died a few weeks after his resignation in January, 1949. He was succeeded by Brigadier Fergus Knox D.S.O., A.D.C., known to his army associates as Gandhi. Under his command and that of his successor Brigadier Ian Good D.S.O., standards of drill, shooting and equipment and turnout steadily improved. Puttees and the old khaki web equipment with wide shoulder straps and pouches for fifty rounds disappeared. The cut of tunics and trousers improved. Black buttons replaced brass.*

Monsoon cloaks instead of groundsheets were issued for wet night patrols. Compulsory retirement of all ranks at 60, with a possible extension to 65, was introduced, but still does not apply to those who joined before 1947. These old hands are free to stay on as they feel fit to do so. The force slowly and inevitably, to a good many perhaps regrettably, from top to bottom became more professional.

Nevertheless each Sub-District remains and rightly so, more or less of a private army, proud of its own particular way of doing things. This outlook is encouraged by the almost complete absence of inter-district

---

* Methods and equipment vary from County to County. Some Londonderry City Area Platoons still retain brass " Derry City " shoulder badges. This area also retained bayonets until the last decade. In Londonderry City itself up until a few years ago, the Platoons were grouped in Companies, with Company Commanders and Company Sergeant-Majors, a survival of the original U.V.F. organisation.

contact.\ The members of the rifle teams meet briefly twice a year at competitions but this of course, only applies to a minority and the remainder train and patrol quite separately. There is no mess life such as the T.A. have and no consultative or representative body.

The Maghera District, now known as No. 3 again, kept well abreast of these post war developments. Major Harry Clark, ably assisted by S/I. Jack Darragh, who had succeeded S/I. McMillan at the end of the war put the Annual Inspections onto a competitive basis which produced a keen interest in drill and turn out. In the shooting sphere Upperlands and Tamlaght sub-districts failed to find their pre-war form and the honours went round from year to year but after 1950 we did not capture the County Cup so regularly as in the past.

In 1953 a contingent of Specials from Ulster went to London for the Coronation and Coronation Medals were awarded to S.D.C. T Johnstone J.P. and Pl/Sergt. Crowe.

In 1954, Mr. Alex McMullan, M.M., M.S.M., succeeded George Evans as Adjutant. George is still, in 1966, a frequent and popular visitor at County and District functions. A year later, Col. R. W. H. Scott, O.B.E., D.L., J.P., was appointed as County Commandant, Captain Lenox-Conyngham having retired due to ill health.

The new officers soon absorbed the family spirit of the force as the two following stories which they like to tell against themselves will show.

One evening shortly after his appointment, Mr. McMullan when inspecting a sub-district observed one of the men wearing a pair of shiny brown shoes. Not wishing to embarrass him he asked quietly, " Would you not have a nice pair of black shoes or boots at home?" " Why " said the culprit, " are ye looking a pair?"

On the other occasion the new County Commandant came to inspect a practice emergency call-out. The men of Tamlaght were not supposed to have been told of the night or time of the call-out and Colonel Scott was slightly surprised two minutes after the message had been telephoned through to meet S/C. Smith Nelson, then aged well over 60, walking fully uniformed and armed to join his section. " That's quick work," he said, " you wouldn't have had any warning of the call-out, would you?" Smith put his hand on the Colonel's shoulder and advised him not to be asking any silly questions and just go to his bed.

In 1955, S/Sergt. H. W. S. Clark was appointed Maghera District Commandant.

Shortly after this S/I. Jack Darragh was tragically killed in a motor accident near Maghera. He was held in particularly high regard throughout the District and a cup for plate shooting bearing his name, purchased by general subscription is now competed for each year.

From 1954 onward, I.R.A activity began to increase, encouraged by a fresh anti-partition campaign. The month of June saw Armagh Depot successfully raided for rifles. In October the same game was tried at Omagh but an alert sentry gave the alarm and several I.R.A. men were captured the local U.S.C. playing an outstanding part. Later came an equally unsuccessful raid at Roslea Police Barracks. A splinter group of the I.R.A. blew a hole in the wall, and attempted to enter, but were driven back in confusion by the gallantry of Sergt. Morrow with a Sten gun. Con Green the I.R.A. leader was shot dead.

Then the surprising results in the 1955 General Election when Sinn Fein candidates in Ulster received 150,000 votes made it possible to believe that Northern Ireland was ripe for liberation. The I.R.A. began to plan greater things. In the winter of 1954-55 the Maghera District started road patrols, the first for eight years. These took the form of four hour spells but in full sections not half ones as during the war and often in areas well away from home.

The year was marked for the District by two outstanding exercises in co-operation with the R.U.C. Reserve Force from Belfast, one near Cookstown and another at Toome aerodrome. The Reserve Force men led by District Inspector Bob Winder, were as fine a crowd as one could wish to meet, somehow managing to combine the dash of good soldiers with the more serious attitude to life of the policeman. The Maghera District acted as assault force at the Toome exercise and some of them crossed the Moyola River at midnight by boat while Helen Clarke, the S.D.C.'s daughter, used her charms to divert the attention of the enemy's sentries. The Reserve Force reported that she played this part with great enthusiasm, and the exercise was enjoyed by all, except by the ' B ' man who jumped into a full water tank thinking it would be a good dry place in which to hide.

S.D.C. Jim Clarke of Upperlands was awarded the B.E.M. in June that year shortly before he retired.

His early death in December, 1956 was a blow to all who knew him, for his shrewdness and hard work had played a great part in building up the efficiency of the post. He had appeared in Six County Final Shoots on no less than six occasions and won many individual prizes with the rifle.

The U.S.C., after many years of negotiation were at last recognised in England to the extent of being allowed to qualify for the Special Constabulary Long Service Medal and about 40 members of the District had the necessary fifteen years qualification. This was much appreciated; of one local man it was said he'd sooner have the medal than a farm o'land.

Old Harry Clark, the first D.C. died on 30th May, 1956. He had kept his ready wit and interest in the U.S.C. right until the end. A few months before his death he was attending the funeral of an old ' B ' man but when someone asked him if he was going to the graveside he said, " No, they might try and put me in too to save time! "

Chapter 9

MURDER BY NIGHT

Whenever there was fighting,
Or a wrong that needed righting,
An Ulster man was sighting,
His long brown gun with care.
                                    W. F. Marshall.

KILLYTONEY who have a special reputation for alertness, had a patrol out on the Draperstown/Magherafelt Road, on the night of 11th December 1956, a date which came to be well remembered.

At midnight as everything appeared normal the Killytoney men stood down but some of them while going to bed heard two cars pass through at high speed, having come from the direction of the mountains.

About 1 a.m. the D.C. was awakened by S/I. Bogle M.M. shouting at his window. "Balloon's gone up, Sir, Balloon's gone up!" He added that Magherafelt Barracks had been burned down and that there was trouble all over the country. Messages were got to the outlying Sub-Districts by various means and within an hour every man was on duty; the first call out for fifteen years! More than half the district's rifles were away with the armourer for their annual overhaul, but the 'Bs' turned out with added zest carrying an interesting collection of private weapons from shotguns to U.V.F. Martinis.

"Tell Mr. Wallace the Innisrush boys are on the job," was one of the messages that came through to the D.C.'s home just after he had gone out that night, a comforting one to those who had to sit there and wait, and to whom it seemed that all hell was let loose on the countryside. The 'Bs' were busy setting up road check points, some near home, others in remote Nationalist areas. Rumours, mostly of enemy success, circulated freely but in the morning as proper reports began to come in, it seemed that the night which was to have been a dramatic start to the great New Campaign had gone badly for the I.R.A. Five of their men were in police lock-ups, three caught at Torr Head Radar Station, two at Armagh Military Depot. Magherafelt Barrack had not been attacked; a garbled report had confused it with the Courthouse which was slightly damaged; no success of any consequence had been achieved in ten separate operations. Yet the terrorists had achieved a degree of surprise which would be impossible again for many years. Even the most unimaginative during the nights that followed must have sensed the tension over the whole countryside as thousands of pairs of eyes stared into the darkness on the look-out for the enemy. Every loyal man or woman in Ulster seemed to contribute his or her share to the total sum of watchfulness.

The next two nights each produced a call out of the District. One, an unsuccessful attempt to intercept a Flying Column in Glenshane Pass, and the other in the form of an ambush to await an attack on Draperstown Barracks. At Draperstown it was as wild a night as I have have ever been out on; a great gale was blowing with the near full moon flicking in and out from behind the clouds. Exactly at the time we had been told to expect the attack, a vehicle halted outside the Barrack and everyone's fingers tightened on the trigger. The previous night we had found out afterwards that there had been no firing pin in the Bren—this time there was no mistake . . . . men got out and approached . . . we watched every move . . . suddenly the moon shone full. It was a group of teddy boys back from a dance! Two hours later stiff, cold and sleepy we drove home for a few minutes in bed before the day's work.

What did the enemy hope to achieve?

A few days later documents detailing I.R.A. plans were captured by the Garda Siochana and were read out in Court in Dublin. They went as follows: "*Phase One. One month: Destruction of listed targets . . . T.A. post in Magherafelt; seizing the Dungiven R.U.C. post blocking the main Belfast/Derry Road at Glenshane Pass . . . . Destruction of local R.U.C. unit and U.S.C. range at Ballyronan. Blow bridges across the Bann at Toome, Newferry and Portglenone.*"

Even the I.R.A. must have their bureaucrats for the bridge at Newferry is non-existent and the ferry stopped operating forty years ago!

"*Phase Two*" was to be "*one month build-up period,*" and *Phase Three* was vaguer still. "*Continuation of struggle onto a higher level when we can co-ordinate on a more perfect communication basis.*" "*In time,*" it was also stated, "*as we build up our forces we hope to liberate large areas, that is areas where the enemy's writ no longer runs.*"

Uniformed Flying Columns of 25 men armed with Brens, Stens and Rifles were to operate from mountain bases, cut all communications, destroy petrol stations and strike at enemy supplies and administrative centres.

The R.U.C. Reserve Force was much too busily occupied elsewhere to assist locally and during the next few weeks while more platoons were being formed, the extra work fell heavily on the 'Bs.' There were daytime sweeps with the local police as well as patrolling by night. Many new members were rapidly recruited including a high proportion of ex-servicemen who in peaceful times do not comprise more than about 10% of the District. The most lively of the new men was Captain Dick Clark who had seen much active service during the war as a Sapper and began a short but colourful career as a Special Constable, U.S.C. on 17th December.

Sunday 23rd December produced a record breaking total of three emergency call outs for the District. At 0230 Swatragh was reported "under attack." A party of Upperlands men including the D.C. were the first support to reach the Barrack but were too late to intercept the enemy. Five shots had been fired through the back of the building, one of which pierced the water tank so that the ground floor was flooded when we arrived but there was no other damage or casualties.

Captain Dick, not yet issued with uniform appeared clad in paint-stained overalls, Sten-gun in hand, and the Magherafelt tender crew who came in twenty minutes later were certain they had got an I.R.A. man in their sights when they met him at the lower end of the town. They closed in in a tight circle with Sten guns trained at his tummy, but luckily did not open fire. H/C. Gregg of Coleraine was also soon on the spot and hasty

MURDER BY NIGHT 103

consultation took place on the subject of recognition between our own forces.

At 4 p.m. the same day, the D.C. was in Draperstown on his way round the District to distribute the extra Sten guns which had been quickly made available when a report was received that the I.R.A. were out in force in Dreenan. The ten miles to Upperlands were covered in approximately 10 minutes and a mobile car column was hastily organised heading from there for the area, while another led by S.D.C. John Patterson started out from Tamlaght. But if the enemy were out they eluded us, for all we found was a Gaelic football team climbing into a bus.

At 8.30 p.m. that night came the news of an attack on Dungiven Barracks. Patrols from the District first blocked Glenshane Pass then sent a party into town where they met D.I. Harold Wolseley. Seventeen tommy-gun bullets had been fired at the Barrack door but there had been no casualties.

It would be tedious to attempt to recall all the incidents of this sort which took place during the winter and one that followed it. The District under the energetic guidance of Col. Bobby Scott, the County Commandant, did its best to retain the initiative by constantly changing the pattern of patrolling. There were road check point patrols home and away, barrack patrols in Swatragh, Maghera and Draperstown, prowler patrols, bicycle patrols, mobile patrols in cars, ambush patrols, stand-by patrols, decoy patrols and forestry patrols. We were issued with an official motor-cycle for despatch riding which was used by S/C. Robert Ballantyne. The D.C. and

S.D.C. Douglas carried out aerial reconnaissance in army light aircraft. If the enemy had come up the rivers in submarines we'd have gone after them with home made depth charges! That was the spirit but most of the results were negative.

Road patrols stopped cars and cyclists as well as pedestrians but were not much concerned with technical offences like defective lights. "Where are you going?" would often be the opening question. "Out on my ceily," was the expected reply from a mountainy man, bent on an evening visiting friends. Stopping such people was dull, often distasteful work, for most of those quizzed were friendly but the deterrent effect was tremendous and made it impossible for the I.R.A. to organise any large scale operation. Once " on the grapevine" we got a back-handed compliment—a comment from an I.R.A. sympathiser "They can do nothing in Maghera for the 'Bs' are far too active!"

Desertmartin was still the post most feared by the I.R.A. who remembered 1922. Within a two mile radius of that village no incidents occurred throughout the campaign. Maghera post had an awkward often lonely job of providing one and two man escorts for the police vehicles, as their men lived nearest to the Barrack.

Captain Dick became famed for his speed, not always combined with accuracy. There was the night he drove to Dungiven "seventeen miles in eighteen minutes," with Bren, Sten and Rifles poking out of the side windows, to find that the call had been from Dungannon, 40 miles in the opposite direction! The time he carried out practical experiments at high speeds with his jeep

Church Parade, Maghera, 1958

[Photo by courtesy Moore, Coleraine

Maghera District Church parade, August, 1958, marching past Brigadier I. H. Good, D.S.O., A.D.C. Major H. F. Clark, M.B.E., J.P., at the head of the column on the right, beside the D.C., Mr. H. W. C. Clark.

Stand Down parade of Ulster Home Guard, Magherafelt, January, 1944.

Dug-Out at Slaughtneill, 1958

Find the dug-out—In 1958 this hedgerow in Slaughtneill, near Swatragh, concealed a dug-out.
(Solution on page 127)
Inset—H.C. J. Shephard, of Bangor, standing in the mouth of the dug-out.

Damage to Upperlands U.S.C. Hut, January, 1957.

Maghera U.S.C. Officers

[Photo by courtesy Moore, Coleraine

Maghera District U.S.C. Drill Competition, won by Culnady, September 26, 1964.

Front Row — Head Constable Hamilton, R.U.C. (Inspecting Officer), H. W. S. Clark, D.L. (District Commandant), Lieut.-Colonel R. W. H. Scott, O.B.E., D.L., J.P. (County Commandant), Lieut.-Colonel S. Miskimmin (Staff Officer), S.D.C. J. Patterson, J.P., and Lieutenant Glanton, R.N., Gunnery Officer H.M.S. Sea Eagle (Inspecting Officer).

Back Row—S.D.C.'s R. H. Dripps, J.P., I. Patterson, G. Mawhinney, J.P., A. Clark, W. G. Douglas, J.P., and T. Johnston, J.P.

Guerilla Equipment

Contents of the Slaughtneill Dug-out, 1958.

I.G. Inspecting Maghera

[Photo by courtesy Moore, Coleraine

Sir Albert Kennedy, Inspector General, inspecting Maghera District in August, 1962.
Figures, from left to right — S/C. W. J. Patterson, Sergt. McCaughey, B.E.M., S/C. Desmond Waters, Plt./Sergt. (now S.D.C.) Simpson, Portstewart, I.G., Col. R. W. H. Scott, O.B.E., D.L., J.P., County Commandant.

to see if the Dannert wire we were using for road blocks was effective and another when he blew the muzzle off a Verey Pistol while he and the D.C. were testing it loaded with buckshot as a close range weapon.

On a further occasion he led a patrol, authorised for once by County H.Q., to Slaghtfreedan Lodge at Lough Fea. Similar shooting lodges had been burned on the two previous nights and this one seemed certain to be next on the list. Others, however had the same bright idea. The R.U.C. from Cookstown with Moneymore 'B' men were there first, and when the two parties met only the great presence of mind of the R.U.C. Sergeant in charge saved the situation from becoming lethal.* Captain Dick's dash kept his section on their toes but he was aced one night by S/Sergt. Fred Kyle of Innisrush who went through Dick's patrol at a speed which surprised even that Jehu. "It wouldn't have been any good firing after him," said Dick, "he was going faster than the bullets would have travelled." Sergt. Kyle was on his way to warn S.D.C. McCaughey of the third callout in 24 hours and was wasting no time! He himself was later specially commended by the County Commandant for his keenness in carrying out in a tireless manner many more patrols than the official number.

Captain Billy Clark, ex-Irish Guards, also joined, and at one time assisted by John Kane, ex-R.A.F., built up quite an effective wireless network for the District using ex-Government tank sets.

In January 1957 Major Harry Clark rejoined as a Special Constable and eight months later was appointed unpaid Deputy D.C. S.D.C. John Patterson visited

---

* The lodge stands a few yards on the Tyrone side of the county boundary. This incident led to much closer intercounty liaison in such matters.

patrols all over the District and was extremely active, so, unlike the I.R.A., the 'Bs' had the benefit of leaders who had fought in 1922.

We were short of transport at times. Many regular members of the District, as well as new recruits, Aubrey, Gordon and David Clark, Alex McLean and Andy Smith, generously used their cars as required although there was no indication about how they would be compensated if the vehicles were damaged.

In 1922, it had been the bicycle which allowed I.R.A. Columns to strike at places fifty miles apart on successive nights; now the car gave them even greater mobility. This was one of the main differences from the pre-war days and the situation was complicated in the early stages by the Suez crisis which meant that petrol was rationed for some time. There were also, of course, many more telephones than in 1922 and the I.R.A. surprisingly left the lines uncut for most of the time, so that callouts could be much more quickly organised than in the old days of telegrams and runners.

Yet for all this activity, the new campaign, as compared with 1922 seemed a "phoney" war, for casualties remained providentially light and normal life almost uninterrupted.

Perhaps the most unpleasant aspect of the campaign was not what the I.R.A. actually did but the fear of what they might do.

In the past they had adopted policies of widespread assassination and the fear that they might do so again was always in the minds of those who stayed at home on the winter nights when the men were out on patrol.

In County Tyrone Sergt. Ovens, R.U.C., was lured to

an empty farmhouse by a fake telephone call and there killed by a booby trap. Later Constable Anderson was shot dead on the Border a few minutes after he had said goodnight to his girlfriend.

On 14th January 1957, a bomb was placed against the corrugated iron wall of the Upperlands U.S.C. Hut, close to where several men sat talking round the stove, after a private airgun practice. Only the alertness of S.D.C. Willie Douglas, who heard the retreating I.R.A. man's footseps and got all hands out of the hut in the nick of time saved heavy casualties.

Had several Upperlands men been killed that night it would have been almost impossible to stop local reprisals. Counter reprisals would doubtless have followed and triggered off similar incidents in other parts of the country. The total casualties which might have resulted make a horrifying speculation. Next day the Reserve Force under H/C. Shepherd accompanied by some Upperlands ' B ' men carried out a house to house search on the mountain face. In a cottage near the Fallalea where one old woman was known to live alone two pairs of dirty boots were observed by the fire.

A glance into the room next door showed two men asleep in a double bed, " What are you doing in there?" roared the Head. " Fighting for Ireland," was the reply. " Well come out and die for Ireland! " Their haversacks contained spare clothing insulating tape, marked maps, an I.R.A. receipt book with several local takings, and last disgrace of the soldier, weapons in rusty condition, a revolver and a commando knife. The simplest lookout or concealment would have given them every chance of escape. They later admitted "off the record" that it was they who bombed the Upperlands hut. No action was taken against their hostess.

S/C. Johnston of Tobermore became the first member of the district to engage the enemy, when on returning from a parade he saw men moving about in the vicinity of electric power lines in Ballinahone. Just as he got off his bike there was a great flash as the lines were shorted and he had time to fire a couple of shots at the fleeing figures. The whole ground was so charged with electricity that when he returned to his bike he found it "live" to touch.

At the end of January 1957 he and four others, the D.C., S.D.C. Willie Douglas, S/Cons. Dick Clark and Alec Patterson, received Favourable Records for good police duty performed in combating subversive activity.

Swatragh Barrack was attacked twice more, in August 1957 and again on the anniversary of the attack on the Upperlands Hut on 14th January 1958. That night the I.R.A. activated some 70 Volunteers, and between 9 and 10 o'clock constructed eleven road blocks, in a ring round the town, ready for a set piece attack on the policemen they were so determined to liquidate.

At 10 o'clock they opened fire from a dark alley opposite the front door of the Barrack, but must have been shaken to find their fire promptly returned by a section, six strong of Upperlands 'B' men who were on duty there inside the circle of road blocks! Half the 'B' men were in the sandbagged enclosure which in those stormy times decorated the front of every police barrack and the others a few yards up the street. Commanding the section was S/Sergt. Thomas McCaughey ("Two Gun Tom") one of the best shots in the District.

In the first exchange of fire S/Con. Jim Murray (ex-B.S.M. Coleraine Battery, T.A.) was hit in the eye by a splinter, and S/Con. Billy Burnside got a bullet through his hat in the best cowboy tradition.*

These were part-time policemen who had completed a normal day's work and left their family firesides only a few minutes before. Now they found themselves in the midst of a life and death gun battle. The Police quickly got their Bren gun into action from the upper window of the Barrack, and the sound of long bursts of fire carried far over the countryside through the still warm night. Men from the neighbouring U.S.C. units ran to arms at the sound and as soon as groups of 3 or 4 men assembled got into cars and closed in on Swatragh from all sides. The I.R.A. road block parties had done a feeble job and their work caused little delay.

Meanwhile the gunmen in the alley had swiftly broken off the action and were beating a retreat. S/Sergt. Percy Douglas driven by S/Con. Aubrey Clark and accompanied by S/Con. Willie Campbell formed one of the approaching carloads. As they sped towards the Barrack they challenged a car which met them and when it failed to stop fired a warning shot.

---

* S/Con. Murray subsequently lost the sight of his eye. He and S/Sergt. McCaughey also Constable Stanley McKeown, (one of the regular police in the barrack) were awarded the B.E.M. for their efforts. S/Sergt. Douglas and S/Con. Clark were rewarded Favourable Records for making the arrest.

The car came to a halt and the driver got out. He had a cut on his face and wet clothing so they arrested and took him to the Barrack. " It'll be a long time before the crows dung on that boy," was one ' B ' man's forecast when he saw them arrive. It was.

Meanwhile the R.U.C. and Specials had reached the town from other directions and a cordon was thrown round the area, but no further culprits were captured.

On Easter Sunday 1957 information was received indicating an attack on Maghera Barrack the following night. The D/I. asked for support from the Specials, and several ambush parties were placed around the barrack. It was always easy on these occasions when there was a chance of action to get extra help and Henry Clark (later M.P. for North Antrim) joined us. He was home on leave from Africa, and armed with a pick shaft and wearing his green bush hat, looked like " Saunders of the River." We got into position with stealth and lay there in great expectation. The pedestrians who passed and repassed would have been surprised to know how minutely their movements were observed. At last hours later, reluctantly we gave up and came home. Perhaps it was a fake message, but one could afford to miss no chance of engaging such an elusive enemy.

After the early stages a good deal more help became available locally. Platoons of mobilized ' B ' men were stationed once again in Magherafelt (H/C. Hamilton) and Landmore House (near Aghadowey) (H/C. Shepherd, later H/C. Long).

The Forces of the Crown were in a much stronger

position than in 1920 as the Special Powers Act was already on the Statute Book. It was invoked from an early date to intern known I.R.A. supporters on the principle that prevention was better than cure. Over a hundred men were held at one time in a special section of the Crumlin Road jail but many were released on giving an undertaking to abstain from seditious activities.

The army too began to play a part. The Northumberland Fusiliers stationed at Palace Barrack, Holywood, with a detachment in Derry under Major John Deighton, M.C., were most active and sent Zulu patrols in Landrovers almost nightly into our area They were succeeded in turn by the Duke of Wellington's Regiment with whom the District also established many contacts, Major (now Brigadier) Tony Firth M.C. being particularly helpful. This fine Regiment had just returned from anti-terrorist duties in Cyprus so had much to tell us. Battalion and Company sweeps were carried out on several occasions in the Slaghtneil/ Lisnamuck areas. The soldiers did not enter houses but held the ring for the police. Brigadier Oliver Brooke M.C. in command of the 39th Brigade was extremely keen on co-operation, and at one time lent us walkie-talkie sets which were fine until we found the messages coming through on Television!

One snowy morning in February 1957 the D.C. was invited to meet the Brigadier at Swatragh Barracks. On his arrival an excited group were looking at aerial photos taken by the R.A.F. which showed tracks leading to a small wood in Corlecky; human tracks for sure—it must be a dugout! We drove in that direction until the vehicles stuck in a snow drift then took a lane for a mile or so in a curious little procession; three black bullocks that we couldn't get past led the way followed by the Brigadier, in British Warm, brass hat and red tabs, his Brigade Major, D/I. Fred White, three policeman with sterling guns and the D.C. Two more bullocks annoyed at being parted from their chums in front brought up the rear! At last we got to the spot . . . . to find that a farmer had been using the wood to feed hay to his cattle, and made all the tracks himself. But we found plenty of real dugouts later on.

A very close liaison was built up with the regular police too. D.I.s Shea and White at Magherafelt and Coleraine and their successors Durkan and Armstrong became sound friends but closest of all to the 'B' men was Sergt. (now H/C.) Robert Murdoch of Maghera who developed a great reputation for fearlessness also Det. Sergt. (now H/C.) Mick Slevin of Maghera and Det. Con. Ernie Allan in Garvagh. Con. Billy Clingan was the man the 'Bs' saw most of, for he drove the Maghera tender and could always be relied on to be just as good natured at 4 a.m. as at 4 p.m. something which can be said for very few. Sergts. Heslip and Hutchinson who in turn had the lonely job of holding Swatragh Barracks, also won the 'B' men's respect and liking.

As the campaign continued it began to become clear that the I.R.A.'s heart was not in the fight. They had fought well on many occasions in the past but now their name came to be associated with timidity and failure. It was soon a stale joke that their initials stood for " I ran away."

"In war," said Napoleon, "it is not men but the man who counts." Collins, De Valera, McBride, the old I.R.A. leaders, had in succession turned to legitimate politics, now the terrorists lacked a man with fire in his belly to lead and direct their attacks. Ulster on the other hand specialises in producing leaders, and for this fight turned up two of her very best. With Lord Brookeborough, the founder of the U.S.C. and honorary County Commandant as Prime Minister, and Sir Richard Pim K.B.E., V.R.D., D.L. as Inspector General, the 'B' men knew that the Government was right behind them and that their efforts were being directed in the best possible way.

Out of the total of thirty attacks on police barracks none were pressed home and in many cases the I.R.A. took to their heels strewing arms and wounded comrades behind them with equal abandon.

The attempt on Brookeborough at 6.55 p.m. on 1st January 1957 proved to be the zenith of these attacks. In a battle lasting ten minutes with explosives, grenades and fire-bombs two I.R.A. men were killed and three wounded.

Later "the boys of the column" began to confine their efforts to minor undefended targets chopping down telegraph poles, or firing a few shots at passing police cars. In Maghera District telephone kiosks, transformers and electric power lines became favourites. When cornered the gunmen often tamely surrendered. The best catch of all, the envy of, and an object lesson for the entire force was when two S/Cs. named Allen sitting by their fireside in Co. Tyrone heard an explosion and made not for the bang, which was an attempt on

Curlough Training Hall, but straight for the nearest bridge across the Border. They were still in plain clothes, with only one rifle and a torch between them but arrived just in time to intercept a brace of fleeing Tommy gunners who promptly dropped their arms and gave themselves up. "Thank God," one of them is reported to have said when he saw the shiny buttons on the jacket of one of his captors (actually a bus conductor's uniform); "Thank God it's the police. I thought it was those bloody 'Bs'! In Maghera District the I.R.A. made eight attempts to blow up bridges a job which their fathers in 1921 had brought to a fine art. Two attempts at Ranaghan locally called David Mary Anne's on Glenshane Pass, two at Dreenan, others at Straw, Curran, Claudy and Lislea. Not a single bridge was rendered impassable to traffic by the puny craters which were made. The lowest ebb was reached when five self styled Freedom Fighters blew themselves to pieces in a cottage just south of the Border as they prepared for a raid on Armagh, thus providing the heaviest casualties of the whole campaign.

Still the guerilla tactics had a nuisance value out of all proportion to their real size, and the I.R.A. did have successes though luckily not in our area. They blew up the new £40,000 Territorial Army Centre at Dungannon two days before it was due to be opened, and a splinter group of which there were several later used £10 worth of gelignite to do £100,000 worth of damage to the lock gates of the Newry Ship Canal. Perhaps their most enterprising effort was to overpower an engine driver and set the train going full speed as a guided missile into the heart of Londonderry's good yard. Luckily, a wide awake signalman switched the points and serious damage was avoided. But these few brilliant pieces of sabotage were not enough in themselves to make the campaign look successful. The bulk of the Nationalists in Ulster made it plain that they were not prepared to outlaw themselves for a lost cause and few gave support in the way of harbouring or providing information which was so vital to the terrorists.

Despite a fiery manifesto published at the end of 1957 which claimed that " anti-British resistance in Ulster is growing stronger," the I.R.A. soon gave up hope of finding a prolonged welcome in nationalist farmhouses. Dugouts were constructed where the gunmen could hide, or store food and arms. No less than nine of these were unearthed in the Maghera District, more per square inch than were found anywhere else in the Province. Two were at Slaghtneil, one at Bragharelly three in Knockoneill, one at Brown's Corner, one at Tamlaght and another in Tirkane. Four of them were big enough for two or more men to live in, the others contained stocks of arms mostly in appallingly rusty condition. There is little evidence that any successful operations were based on these dugouts but there may well be today several more undiscovered close by.

U.S.C. training was improved to meet the situation. A course of night firing for each man was introduced, and firing from the kneeling and standing position included in the Annual Course. In Maghera we devised Mobile Patrol Competitions for sections in cars; these involved removing booby-trapped road blocks following complex routes by 1 in. Map, as well as getting the vehicles over various obstacles. Culnady hold the Shield put up for this Contest.

By 1959 the lost deposits of the Sinn Fein Candidates in the General Election further discouraged the " Freedom Fighters." There were only 19 recorded incidents in that year and 21 in 1960 (none of any importance in the District) out of a total in the campaign of over 600. Strangely enough all the later exploits were attacks on communications within a few yards of the Border. Culverts were blown, and the railway cut on several occasions, actions which divided Ulster physically as well as politically from the rest of Ireland, but we have long ceased to expect logic from the I.R.A. The final straw for them was when Mr. Sean Lemass at last felt strong enough after the 1961 Election in the South to revive the wartime Special Courts which were not afraid to imprison I.R.A. men for long terms. On 26th February 1962 the I.R.A.'s own publicity bureau in Dublin announced the end of the campaign. Arms were said to have been dumped and all units withdrawn across the border. This curious and apparently unnecessary announcement of something which had been obvious for months was almost certainly made in order to obtain the release of the I.R.A. men held by their own government.

Since 1956 the I.R.A. had killed six policeman and special constables and wounded 32 others. The damage caused amounted to £1,000,000 but the cost of security measures was probably considerably higher. Of their own men two were killed in action and seven in

MURDER BY NIGHT

incidents with home made bombs. Forty six I.R.A. men were serving sentences in Belfast gaol convicted of normal criminal charges.

Once again the U.S.C. found themselves at peace and once again wondered how long it would last.

First stage in excavating an I.R.A. dugout at Knockoneil, near Maghera.

Chapter 10

PEACE AT LAST

SINCE 1962 the Maghera 'B' men have not, except for one short period, been called on to do any patrolling. With the rest of the U.S.C. they remain a cheap and efficient deterrent at the immediate disposal of the Ulster Government for use against any renewed attempt at terrorism.

The men mobilized during the trouble to reinforce R.U.C. stations and form extra Reserve Force platoons have been gradually disbanded. Training tends more and more away from the military and towards producing men able to help the R.U.C. in their normal police duties. The aim is to have special constables able to take over as station orderly, to assist with traffic control and at accidents: also to fit into the Civil Defence organisation. In the unthinkable event of "the Bomb" hitting Ulster every uniformed man would be needed to prevent widespread disorder.

All ranks, instead of N.C.O.'s only are now trained in the use of the pistol, a much more suitable weapon than the rifle for these new functions. The force was thankful a couple of years ago to see the end of the wartime Sten sub-machine gun, a weapon highly dangerous to a careless user and his comrades. Now it has the more sophisticated Sterling and Mark IV rifles have replaced the old S.M.L.E. Mark III's many of which were of 1914 vintage. Care of arms is generally good, although there is still the odd lapse as when the D.C. putting his eye to a rifle barrel at Innisrush was surprised to see a large spider glaring back at him! We have come a long way from the old days of the 1920's when a 'B' man arrived proudly home to show off the new rifle he scarcely knew how to work and met objection from his mother, "She's no charged, Ma!" he protested. "Charged or no charged, son she's dangerous; Houl her till the door!"

Brigadier Good has retired from the position of Staff Officer, and Colonel Steve Miskimmin who had been acting as his assistant was appointed in his place. Major Jack Chapman M.C. became the new assistant, and in spite of the Government economy drive these two able administrators have managed to get much new and better equipment for the Force, including the weapons already mentioned. In July 1962, Major Harry Clark the Deputy District Commandant retired. (Possibly for the last time, but if the I.R.A. start up again, everyone will be surprised if he does not find his way back in).

The District were extremely sorry to lose, due to the axing of the staff, the services of "wee Geordie" Hanson, ex-Special Air Services Regiment, small in stature but big in heart, who acted as assistant Sergeant Instructor for several years; but they were lucky indeed to get on 1st November 1960, the best S.I. seen for many years, John Chestnutt ex-C.S.M. of the Irish Guards. His energy, knowledge and sense of humour have won the liking of everyone. In him and S.I. Smith, who looks after Killytoney and Desertmartin sub-districts, Maghera have the best possible regular staff.

At County level Joe Cantley has carried on the good work of Alex McMullan as Adjutant since 1962.

In August 1963 Maghera District had the great honour of being inspected at a Church Parade in Tobermore by the Inspector General, Sir Albert Kennedy. It was greatly appreciated when he afterwards wrote to the D.C. as follows.

" I send my warmest congratulations to you and all who paraded for inspection on a most excellent turnout. It was very obvious to me that all ranks had taken great care and made every preparation for the inspection. Uniforms and equipment were first-class and I had a clear impression that everyone took pride in his appearance. The marching to church was really good and I heard many favourable comments on it.

Altogther, this was a very happy and successful occasion and I have no doubt that the public who were present in large numbers were as favourably impressed as I was."

In 1965 a County drill competition was held for the first time and was won by the District represented by Culnady, S.D.C. Dripps and P/Sergt. Kyle. Later the same year after long delays a new drill Hut in Maghera was opened by Major James Chichester-Clark D.L., M.P., the son of the 1922 Area Commander, and to our great pleasure, Professor R. L. Marshall attended the ceremony. The building is of brick with a wooden block floor and proper toilet facilities, of a standard much better than anything previously supplied for the ' Bs.'

In 1966 came the 50th Anniversary of the Easter Rising. The I.R.A. had elaborate plans to mark the celebrations with terrorism all over the North, and their chances of pulling off a success seemed good. The longer they leave it between attacks, the easier it is for them to make a successful one, as the edge goes off the defenders alertness. However under the expert guidance of Sir Albert Kennedy, the R.U.C. and U.S.C. a few weeks before Easter quietly stood to. Road patrols appeared all over the country and such was the air of preparedness that the I.R.A. scouts must have reported that things would be too hot for anyone who tried to make trouble.

The feeling of comradeship in the 'Bs' which runs so strong in troubled times tends to be lost a little in between, although it is kept alive as far as possible by District Suppers and the like. It is always there under the surface and came strongly out on those cold nights last Easter, when men were out quietly observing and waiting without stopping vehicles or pedestrians. One Tamlaght Patrol had three shots fired at it but the fact that there was no terrorism of any consequence was the greatest tribute to the handling of the situation by the Government and the good use they made of the Constabularies.

It is much easier to be a historian than a prophet and what the future has in store for Northern Ireland is difficult to predict. Every Irishman of good sense hopes for peaceful times throughout the land, and a chance to enjoy the delightful country we live in.

Two things are sure. The first is that the time when extremists on either side of the Border can do their cause any good is long past; and the second that whenever the 'Bs' are needed they will respond to the call and be ready to " make the foes of Ulster rue the day that they were born!'

Upperlands, November 1966.

The I.R.A. dugout at Knockoneil uncovered. Inside rusty small arms were found, but the birds had flown.

ACKNOWLEDGEMENTS

THE idea of writing this history first came a few months ago during a very good party held by Culnady to celebrate winning the County shoot. My father was asked to tell something about the old days and the close interest taken by all present was very noticeable. Since then the object has changed from being a simple collection of anecdotes to an attempt at a composite history.

Lord Brookeborough as well as honouring us with a Foreword kindly contributed information about the early formation of the Forces and some interesting details about County Fermanagh. Sir Richard Pim and Mr. Jim Harvey made some very helpful criticisms. So many members of the District have helped with dates, details and documents that it would be impossible to mention them all; Pl./Sergt. Bob Rainey and S/Sergt. Alex Crockett were particularly helpful. Professor Marshall who now lives in Derry and the Rev. John Brown Lecturer in History at Magee College, Londonderry who were also kind enough to read proofs and make many suggestions. Mr. Joe Burns M.P. wrote an important contribution about Maghera; Evan Burns his brother also checked the proofs. Several members of my family chiefly my father and Mr. Percy Clark have checked or added facts, and my brother Henry contributed much of the political background. At R.U.C. Headquarters Major Jack Chapman was particularly helpful and at County level Mr. Joe Cantley and S/C. James Monteith did some research which produced much useful information. The R.U.C. Photographic Department were extremely helpful in reproducing the illustrations. Mr. George Evans provided information about the U.H.G. Mr. George Boyce of Queen's University helped by searching newspaper files. S/I. Chestnutt has helped in innumerable ways and without his special brand of enthusiasm the work would never have been completed.

My thanks are due to Mrs. George Bambridge, Messrs.

ACKNOWLEDGEMENTS

MacMillan & Co. and Messrs. Methuen & Co. Ltd., for permission to quote from Rudyard Kipling's poems, and to Mr. M. B. Yeats and Messrs. MacMillan & Co. Ltd., for permission to quote from "The Stare's Nest" by W. B. Yeats.

SOURCES

The stories of the earlier local incidents are mainly those I have heard all my life when older men speak about the "Troubles." Of the later Home Guard days and the 1956-61 trouble a good deal of the material is from personal experience. No other book to date has been produced dealing specifically with the U.S.C. or the I.R.A. attacks on Ulster so for information I have had to select from many sources the chief ones being as follows.

Ulster's Stand for Union—McNeill.

The Orange and the Green—King.

The Administration of Ireland in 1920—"I.O." (C. J. C. Street).

No Other Law—O'Donoghue.

With the I.R.A. in the Fight for Freedom—Beaslai.

Guns for Ulster—Col. Fred Crawford.

Files of "Newsletter," "Telegraph," "Northern Constitution."

Finally I am greatly indebted to Miss Margaret Kirkpatrick and Miss Freda Watson without whose expert typing this production would have been impossible.

PRINCIPAL DATES

1904 UNIONIST CLUBS FORMED IN IRELAND.

1912 SIGNING OF ULSTER COVENANT.

1913 ULSTER VOLUNTEER FORCE FORMED.

1914 April—Larne Gun Running.
August—START OF GREAT WAR.
September—Home Rule Bill Passed.

1916 Easter—Dublin Rebellion.

1918 END OF GREAT WAR.

1920 Great I.R.A. activity in south, 193 policemen murdered, Black and Tans, Auxiliary Cadets formed to reinforce R.I.C. U.V.F. re-formed in Ulster.
October 22—DECISION TAKEN TO RAISE SPECIAL CONSTABULARY IN SIX COUNTIES.
December—GOVERNMENT OF IRELAND ACT PASSED. PARTITION SET UP.

1921 January 13—Principal meeting to recruit Maghera District, Special Constabulary.
May—FIRST GENERAL ELECTIONS IN NORTH AND SOUTH.
June 6—Swatragh Ambush. Sergt. Burke shot.
June 19—OPENING OF PARLIAMENT IN BELFAST BY KING GEORGE V.
July 11—TRUCE SIGNED IN IRELAND BETWEEN BRITISH GOVERNMENT AND PROVISIONAL GOVERNMENT OF IRELAND.
December—TREATY SIGNED ESTABLISHING IRISH FREE STATE.

1922 March 19—Moyola Bridge blown up. S. Kirkpatrick shot. Maghera Barrack captured.
March 30—Collins-Craig Pact arranging truce in the North. This lasted a few days only.
May 3—Attacks on Bellaghy and Draperstown Barracks.

May 16—3 policemen shot at Ballyronan.
May 19—Sack of Desertmartin, 4 men shot.
May 24—I.R.A. declared illegal. Great Round Up, 500 Sinn Feiners interned.
June 1—Curfew over whole country.
R.I.C. Disbanding. R.U.C. formed.
June 28—Attack on Four Courts in Dublin. START OF CIVIL WAR IN SOUTH.
December—Inspection of Maghera District by Sir James Craig.

1923 April—END OF CIVIL WAR.

1924 End of Internment in Northern Ireland. 'A' Specials disbanding.

1938 Maghera Riots. I.R.A. attacks in England.

1939 September—START OF SECOND WORLD WAR.

1940 May—FORMATION OF L.D.V.'s, LATER RE-NAMED ULSTER HOME GUARD.

1944 January—HOME GUARD STAND DOWN.

1945 END OF SECOND WORLD WAR.

1954 Raids on Armagh and Omagh Barracks.

1955 150,000 votes recorded for Sinn Feiners candidates in General Election.

1956 December 11—COMMENCEMENT OF NEW I.R.A. CAMPAIGN.
December 23—Attacks on Swatragh and Dungiven Barracks.

1957 August—Second attack on Swatragh Barrack.

1958 January—Third attack on Swatragh Barrack. S/C. Murray wounded. S./Sergt. McCaughey and S./C. Murray awarded B.E.M.

1962 I.R.A. ANNOUNCES END OF CAMPAIGN.

1966 Easter—50th ANNIVERSARY OF DUBLIN REBELLION—GENERAL STAND TO IN ULSTER.

ABBREVIATIONS

I.G.—Inspector General.
D.I.—District Inspector.
C.I.—County Inspector.
D.C.—District Commandant.
S.D.C.—Sub-District Commandant.
H/C.—Head Constable.
P/SGT.—Platoon Sergeant.
S/SGT.—Special Sergeant.
S/C.—Special Constable.
R.I.C.—Royal Irish Constabulary.
R.U.C.—Royal Ulster Constabulary.
I.R.A.—Irish Republican Army.
L.D.V.—Local Defence Volunteers
U.H.G.—Ulster Home Guard.
O/C.—Officer Commanding.
S/I.—Sergeant Instructor.
T.A.—Territorial Army.

The entrance was discovered by H.C. Gregg, who observed that there was no moss on the big stone in the centre of the picture. This covered a vertical shaft to the entrance.

THE SPECIALS SACRIFICED

Postscript to Second Edition. May 2002

'It is a law of life that is yet to be broken that a nation can only earn the right to live soft by being prepared to die hard in defence of its living.'
Field Marshall Wavell 1945

For the half century after 1920 the B Specials were far the strongest in number of the guardians of Northern Ireland. They mustered almost twice as many as the RUC and army combined.

The IRA, as we have seen, admitted on 26 February 1962 that their 1956 Harvest Campaign had been defeated. Shortly afterwards Lord Brookborough, the Premier under whose leadership Ulster had remained stable for twenty years, resigned. He was succeeded by Captain Terence O'Neill whose liberal outlook and steps towards reconciliation coincided with a period of increasing prosperity.

In the Sixties car ownership in Ulster doubled to become the highest per head in all the UK. Between 1950 and 1970 a quarter of the population of Northern Ireland moved into modern homes. Full employment spread steadily outwards from Belfast. The RUC achieved a detection rate of almost 65 % -- so crime was infrequent.

There was still discrimination. Conor Cruise O'Brien summarised this in his recent book Memoirs .' *The Catholics of Northern Ireland suffered from a genuine sense of grievance, and also greatly exaggerated the extent of the same. Stormont had few delegated powers but abused those it had in relation to jobs, housing and local franchise.'*

In Ulster each faction considered that its chosen end justified the means--, the destruction of Ulster as a community by the Republicans, the preservation of the UK link by the Unionists. To achieve results the Republicans favoured violence ; the Unionists, more mildly, exercised selective Local Government gerrymandering. This practice appeared to most of their supporters essential as a means of preserving the State, the first responsibility of any government.

South of the Border in the Irish Republic there was discrimination too and the Protestant population declined according to a recent Northern Ireland Office figure from twenty two percent in 1922 to three percent today.

But in spite of opposing aspirations relations in the Sixties between the communities slowly improved. Such Protestant strongholds as Ballymena and Larne elected popular Catholic Mayors.

After 1962 the B s reverted to Drill Category – that meant 24 training periods a year of drill, tactics, observation and law, plus a musketry course. For this each Special Constable was paid the unprincely sum of £15 a year. Few , if any , operational duties were needed.

In Maghera District we acquired a new Sergeant Instructor in the person of James Bogle. He had won his first Military Medal in Italy when his section captured a German lookout post and the five men in it. When five more Germans came unwittingly as relief Bogle's riflemen overpowered them too and marched the ten prisoners back to Company headquarters . Later he won a bar to his Military Medal in Belgium so we knew him for a man of determination and up to the very high standard of our full time staff .

The affable Lieutenant Colonel Ken Davidson, late the Argyll and Sutherland Highlanders, became County Commandant. He had previously served six years with us as Special Constable and Adjutant, so needed no initiation.

Terence O'Neill had meetings with Lemass and Lynch, the Dublin Premiers. Cooperation increased between Governments north and south of Border.

The mid Sixties were a time of optimism when the people of Ulster, except the few haters at each extreme, had reason to feel that they'd never had it so good.

There seemed a real possibility of the fighting being over and that Ulster, if left free from outside agitators, could resolve her problems.

What older residents now find so galling when they look back is the way this euphoric period turned so swiftly to bitter strife.

The reasons for this change can be summarised as follows.

Internationally The Sixties were a decade of challenge to authority.

Protesters marched in the Champs Elysee in Paris and Little Rock, USA.

In Grosvenor Square, London, nine thousand policemen were required to control the agitators on a later occasion. It was also an age when most wars, like that in Ireland could be defined as separist. Numerous communities - the Basques in Spain, the French Canadians in Quebec, the coloured tribes of Africa and minority groups within the emerging European Union sought independence.

Media pressure was another factor. Our problems in Ulster were too familiar at home to need headlining but groups in England were all too keen continually to draw attention to them. A French naval friend remarked to me at the time, 'Half your nations are heroes, the rest are swine'. He referred to the factions in England always ready to support their country's enemies of any colour or creed.

Television too had its malignant effect. It was still a novelty and had as such a disproportionate influence. Programmes highlighted strife and bloodshed. Peace and reconciliation were given minimum cover. The way in which violence appeared to be celebrated and social jealousies emphasised assisted left wing activists.

In the middle of the Sixties came the Fiftieth Anniversary of the 1916 Rising. I recall hoping that once this was duly triumphalised, The Troubles might be allowed to sink into the past and that we could begin jointly to enjoy Ireland's matchless heritage and unspoiled countryside. How wrong I was. The 1916 Celebrations instead provided a grandstand for renewed Republican calls to end Partition. But the bombings and shootings with which the IRA had intended to draw international attention to the occasion were a non-event. They were quietly thwarted in a massive alert by RUC and USC.

It was at this stage that *Guns in Ulster* was first published. The name was chosen because Ulster had been at that time at peace for a lustrum, the book theme is historical and guns were beginning to seem a thing of the past.

In about 1966 a new generation of clever Nationalist agitators was emerging. Their howls of protest gave rise in turn to the public appearances of Ian Paisley whose booming voice and flair for publicity convinced hearers that bigotry in Ulster was rife.

Catholics soon realised his value to their cause.

. About this time in the snug of a bar near Portglenone a Republican group was discussing the situation. They were overheard by two off duty Culnady USC Constables next door as they described Paisley as, 'The best man for us since Wolfe Tone. Let's drink till him.'

To sum up-- The Sixties were a decade of protest and provocation when democratic governments learned that it was much more difficult to impose authority than flout it. The factors behind the slide to violence have been well detailed in a unpublished paper by my brother Henry Clark MP. *The Sources of the Troubles in Ulster 1960 – 1970.* As Westminster MP for North Antrim he had ringside seat.

The achievements of the Specials and of how their reputation came to be disparaged by carefully fabricated lies and skilful innuendo is told in with great clarity by Admiral Sir Arthur Hezlet in

The 'B' Specials. *ISBN 1-902 010 –00 – 4 . Mourne River Press, 1997).*

I have quoted by kind permission from both this and my brother's material.
In 1967 the Northern Ireland Civil Rights Association (NICRA) was formed for peaceful protest. .Many Catholics and not a few Protestants of good intent joined NICRA to assist in establishing equal rights. Their activities seemed not unwelcome as it was the first Catholic-led concerted political action in fifty years. Left to develop peacefully it might have led without bloodshed to consensus government. NICRA was however taken over branch by branch as the Irish Republican Army inserted their men into key positions. The NICRA shopping list was now topped by demands for the removal of the B Specials.

This aspiration by men of violence was not surprising, as at about this time Sinn Fein historian Tim Pat Coogan awarded the Specials their best ever compliment .

'The one rock on which any mass movement by the IRA
in the North inevitably foundered.'

In 1968 NICRA marches and protests became more frequent. The RUC while diverting a banned march in Derry were provoked into wielding batons. Some constables raised them above their shoulders where television cameras could record each stroke.Worldwide accusations of brutality followed.

Those of us who holidayed regularly in the Republic knew that the Garda down south were no slouches when it came to baton work. But that of course didn't count .

In rural areas of south Derry peace continued more or less unbroken. As security manpower became stretched in towns and cities the Maghera B Specials carried out local patrols to release RUC men for riot control. We also at times maintained a force of two platoons in Maghera RUC Station in reserve lest trouble should be incited locally. As a group they were not called on .

The rush of Ulster's Gadarene Swine began in 1969.

NICRA initiated a 'Long March' from Belfast for Derry starting on 1st January The object at first seemed unclear but was soon unveiled as a deliberate attempt to provoke violent reaction.

When the RUC re-routed the March round Maghera serious rioting took place. The leaders were carrying tricolor flags, at that time banned in Northern Ireland.

The USC was not involved because, it was said, they lacked training and equipment for riot control. Two frustrated local Special Constables in plain clothes and not on duty were caught up in the fighting. Identified by Nationalists they were later fined in a Magistrate's Court and required to resign.

The marchers were then warned by the RUC that serious opposition awaited them in Derry City but refused to turn aside. On January 4th in a sunken road near Burntollet Bridge three miles short of the City their ranks were broken by volleys of stones. Thirteen footsore marchers were injured; several were taken to hospital. This appeared to be just what the leaders had wanted.

But most of the column, assisted by the RUC, straggled into the City .There another dozen received cuts and blows. The USC took no part.

The aftermath provides a good example of the attempts made to discredit the B men.

Mr Paddy Devlin, Northern Ireland Labour MP for Falls, between 6th May and 8th July 1969 asked no less than 442 questions of Robert Porter, the Minister of Home Affairs. He produced 180 names, allegedly from photographs taken at the incident, and asked the Minister if they were members of the USC. Of these 117 had never been in the USC ; 47 had been members in the past but were not serving at the time. Some had been out for years. Twenty five of the names were serving members but there was only evidence that two were at Burntollet .One who lived nearby was watching 250 yards away from the bridge. The other was not known to have acted unlawfully in any way.

In spite of these answers a disappointed Mr. Devlin repeated his allegations in a debate on the adjournment, saying that a hundred members of the USC were present at the affray.

This statement re-appeared in print in a book under the title *Burntollet*
On the day of the incident Robin Chichester-Clark, Westminister MP for the area, was in Derry. Returning home after the scrummage he stopped at Burntollet to clear bedsteads and stones off the road and was there photographed.

On 17 June Paddy Devlin asked, 'On what date and in which area was Mr Chichester- Clark attested as a Special Constable and rank does he hold?' Also 'Have Police inquiries had established that Robin Chichester was present at Burntollet on 4th Jan 1969?'

To these queries the Minister replied that the gentleman was never attested to the USC and no police inquiries were needed as it was well known that he had visited Burntollet <u>after</u> the disturbances.

It was significant that none of these inquiries asked whether any of the people concerned were members of the Ulster Protestant Volunteers or Ulster Volunteer Force. It was the B men Mr. Devlin aimed to discredit.

Writers like Ludovic Kennnedy, Antony Beevor and Richard Needham who should have been better informed later took up the theme and made pejorative reference to the luckless Specials.

A suggestion that the USC was used officially or deliberately to support attacks on civil rights demonstrations is utterly false and was refuted in the lengthy Cameron Report on the incidents. The B Men wore black uniform and being part-timers with jobs and families to care for by day were generally only available for duty at night. This made it easy for detractors to present them as bogeymen.. In real life they were like the Royal Navy a 'silent service', having no public relations, no Press Officer, not even an Association to represent them. And that was their Achilles heel.

The Burntollet affair was only the beginning of a mendacious campaign against the USC which due to the skill of Republican propaganda was widely believed of the North, in the Republic of Ireland and also in Great Britain.

The Sunday Times Insight team later repeated the untrue allegation that that a hundred B men were identified as taking part in the ambush at Burntollet.

The IRA knew that if you tell big enough lies loudly and repeatedly people will begin to believe them.

So I make no apology for repetition here of the real situation to help to set the record straight.

The USC was not used in crowd or riot control before July 1969. The suggestion that the USC was used officially or deliberately to support attacks on Civil Rights demonstrations is utterly false and has been refuted by the Cameron Committee .

Paddy Devlin's clumsy effort was reminiscent of an earlier fabrication --

laughable if the background was not so deadly serious. Dan Breen, a bold IRA leader of 1922, was getting clear after an attack in County Louth with two fellow Volunteers. They moved at high speed facing outwards in a side car. The road was bumpy. Dan fell out so heavily that his colleagues took him for dead.

'Let's put a few bullets into him ', said one of his companions , 'dump him north of the Border and say there's been a B Special atrocity'.

At this juncture Dan came to and while applauding the idea suggested they find another victim..

As 1969 wore on NICRA led a series of provocative demonstrations and riots . Men with long memories rated them the worst since Northern Ireland was first set up in 1922.

The day after the Twelfth of July 1969, when all Ulster was on holiday, trouble arose in Dungiven. A Republican mob attacked two tenders carrying twenty regular police and reservists. The detachment was almost overwhelmed and took refuge in the Orange Hall they had been sent to protect .

Later they fought their way out and reached the Police Station which stands half way up the hillside on which the town is situated. It in turn was besieged while another part of the mob set about burning the Orange Hall.

The County Inspector was obliged to call out the Limavady B men . Fifty of them quickly assembled at the nearby farm of their District Commandant.

Here on RUC instructions they left their firearms under guard. Batons were issued but no riot shields – these were not at that time generally available. The B men entered Dungiven at the bottom of the town. In attempting to move half a mile up hill to relieve the RUC Station they were assaulted by the mob with taunts, and stones. Later shots were fired at them from a Point 22 rifle. Finding his men in a dangerous position the Commandant sent for the revolvers of his officers and sergeants. Some fifteen shots had to be fired over the heads of the crowd before it began to clear the way. But it was slow work and the detachment did not reach the Police Station until 3 am . Then with the aid of the RUC they cleared the streets and restored order.

The steadiness and discipline of the B men during this long night of violence was beyond reproach. They were warmly congratulated by the County Inspector and set a high standard for future operations . Some men from Maghera District USC who had been mobilized for full time service had played a stout part.

This was just the sort of assistance to the RUC that the B men were there to provide. Although not formally trained for crowd control they had demonstrated their ability to do the job. With some swift re-training they could have done much more. But no such schooling took place in County Derry and I have seen no record of it anywhere else.

The month of August 1969 saw the RUC drawn into battle in Derry with Nationalist rioters who were determined to prevent the traditional Apprentice Boys Parade. Public and private buildings were burned as stoning and fire bombing raged for two long days and nights. For the outnumbered policemen, lacking reserves, it was non stop duty . They had water cannon and tear gas but no relief and no respite. By Day Four 94 policemen had been injured and the remainder were exhausted.

The BBC, not usually noted for pro-police attitudes, reported ;

'The RUC have been magnificent. It is difficult to explain how they have managed to keep their tempers'.

The Derry City USC were used to stop access to the walled city by blocking Castle Gate and Butcher's Gate. They also protected public buildings and guarded Catholic pubs in Protestant areas.

. Maghera District again guarded local Police Stations and patrolled locally under RUC control. Preparing for what might lie ahead we laid in a stock of riot shields, home made but almost indistinguishable from the official models.

On 14th August a call went out on BBC Radio that all USC men were to report at local police stations armed for duty. I was on a sailing holiday in Scotland with my wife and young sons and had to make an overnight passage home in thick fog. On arrival in Portrush at dawn expecting to hear of Province-wide mayhem I was told that no additional effort by the Maghera District was immediately needed. The mobilization was in part a legal preliminary, neeeded before the NI Government could call for help from the army. That day there was a further attack on Dungiven Police Station and similar incidents in towns all over the Province

In Derry The Prince of Wales' Regiment moved as requested into the edge of the Nationalist Bogside. They were welcomed as saviours with smiles and cups of tea but did not attempt to enter the Bogside itself. This honeymoon proved as short as the political strings were long.

The rioting in West Belfast meanwhile was appalling. Specials were used to control Protestant as well as Catholic crowds.

The Republicans were given full scope at this time for heavily biased statements on Television . There was no individual or Government effort to refute them.

A quotation by Sir Arthur from Miss Bernadette Devlin's book illustrates the theme,
' *In Belfast the B Specials alongside the Police fought the demonstrators . They did more. With small arms, machine guns and armoured cars they launched a vicious well planned attack on Catholic areas They burned down row upon row of houses.* '

The B men could not have machine-gunned Catholic houses from armoured cars.

They had neither mounted machine guns or armoured vehicles. For the Specials there was no means of appeal – no spokesman to give instant rebuttal.

The Scarman Tribunal which much later investigated the August fighting shows that there is a scarcely a word of truth in such Nationalists statements but this kind of propaganda seems to have been believed in London by Mr Wilson and Mr Callaghan. On Derry the Scarman Tribunal stated -

'*There is nothing to justify any general criticism of the USC during the few hours it performed riot duty in Londonderry.*'

Shortly after the Army moved in the elected Londonderry Council was suspended on orders from Westminster. A Commission was appointed to run the City on the lines demanded by NICRA.

Labour ministers in London had no experience of local violence, knew little about counter measures and could think of nothing but appeasement

Premier Harold Wilson was naïve enough to believe that a few quick concessions would buy off the terrorists and produce peace - at least until the General Election he planned in 1970 . He announced on television on 22 August-- off the cuff and without having checked its record --- that the Ulster Special Constabulary would be phased out.

The Derry Citizen's Defence Association at once stepped up its demands .Its daily Newsletter Number Eleven (of which I retain a copy) includes :

' *Item 7*

A military supervisory watch to be maintained over Ulster Special Constabulary arms storage. The military to control the issue of these arms.

Item 9

No USC to be used within the City or anywhere west of the Foyle.
This is what the military promised to do if we took down the barricades.
The Defence Association refused the terms for a number of reasons
...---The fact that the barricades are a protection against attack from any quarter.
The fact that our holding this area is the symbol of our continous struggle against the Unionist Government. We hold 888 acres and two roods.
Within this are 25,000 people'.

Copies of the single smudged sheet were available from eight centres in shops, schools and pubs. This indicated the extent to which citizens were arming while the IRA remained at a low ebb in men and equipment.

Wilson's statement about disbandment was promptly denied by the Stormont Government.

Ian Freeland, the General Officer Commanding Northern Ireland, now given overall control of Security, had apparently not been consulted and made a similar denial. He realized the value of the B men in crowd control where sheer weight of numbers often counts most.

Alarmed at Mr.Wilson's outburst the part-time B Special officers got together to attempt to counter the allegations. Leaders were District Commandants Harry Kennedy, primary school headmaster from Belfast, Willie Beatty, farmer from Antrim, Michael Armstrong, QC from Armagh, John Brown, Presbyterian Minister and academic from Derry City, Billy Dixon, farmer from Fermanagh, and myself. They comprised as reasonable and determined a group of men as any with which I have been associated.

. The first meeting took place on 30 August in the Tobermore B Hut, chosen because it was a central point. In attendance on subsequent occasions were the Prime Minister James Chichester Clark (later Lord Moyola) and John Taylor MP. Funds were volunteered for posters and press releases. Editors were lobbied for coverage .

One happy outcome was an undertaking to write a book . This, as mentioned above, was from Admiral Sir Arthur Hezlet DSO ,DSC, a retired submarine ace and international historian of distinction . He started at once to assemble the record of the USC and did so with high accuracy and remarkable speed.

Sir Arthur had plenty to go on. The B Men's wide coverage, sharp eyes and ears to the ground, comprised an intelligence network that made it very difficult for the IRA to assemble for operations, or even plan them, without the authorities being made quickly aware . Another measure of efficiency was their excellent Skill at Arms.

In the Northern Ireland Command Rifle Meeting in April 1968 nineteen teams took part representing the Regular Army, Territorial Army, RAF, RUC and USC. The USC took first, second, and third prizes. It was the first time since 1897 when the competition began that the top prize the Queen Victoria Trophy had been won by other than an army team.

Next was their sheer economy in men and money.

In 1967 the estimates to support 12,500 B Specials were under £ 750,000 .

The Force was administered by less than 75 full time staff. As a proportion of teeth to tail I have not yet to hear of a match.

A total strength of 12,500 meant 12, 400 trained riflemen available for security duties. No men were absorbed in guarding their own headquarters . The B's had none. They made do with rooms inside Police Stations which were already guarded. For their own use they had a few bare training huts which only required a guard when occupied in evenings. Headquarter Guards were to absorb up to 25 % of the strength of their successors the Ulster Defence Regiment.

USC weapon security was good   In 50 years after 1920 USC had lost only 20 weapons. The Army in the same period from their armouries had lost hundreds--300 in one raid alone from Armagh Barracks .

During the fifty years civilians killed by the USC in accidental shooting numbered less than a dozen, an average of one every six years. Sad that was but compare that with later events when the army killed more civilians in Derry one afternoon. In 1972 civilians killed by combatant forces numbered 133 .

Deaths of USC members at the hands of terrorists were seven only between 1922 and 1970. B men knew how to look after themselves and their weapons The IRA had become victims of their own propaganda and quite wrongly pictured every B Specials as a Gestapo type trigger-happy killer. Scared to attack the USC, they might be said to have been stewing in their own juice.

My grandfather 'Hellfire Hal ', my father and myself all received death threats while commanding the District but no serious attempt appeared to have been made to carry them out. Many other B men could tell similar stories.

Anti-propagandists fastened on the fact that the USC contained very few and at times no Roman Catholics. This was in spite of substantial efforts early on recruit them. The effort failed because the IRA showed their determination to murder any Catholic who joined --the old Republican game of refusing cooperation and then crying discrimination.

The IRA boasted at times of their success in infiltrating all departments of Government and branches of the armed forces . The B Specials were never infiltrated.

The Orange Order

One myth de-bunked by Sir Arthur Hezlet is that the Specials *'could not have been formed without the Orange Order and were controlled by the Orange Order'* . This theory may have arisen because in 1913 a pair of Orange Lodges formed the basis for the original Ulster Volunteer Force recruited to counter   Home Rule.

The USC were in no way controlled by the Orange Order . The structure of the Orange Order is entirely unsuitable to exercise such a function .

Some B men were members of the Order , some were not ; it made no difference. The B men drilled in Orange Halls because no other accommodation was available and that was in my area the limit of the connection. In the Maghera District we sometimes drilled in a barn belonging to the Tamlaght SDC, in a railway Goods Shed, a factory dye house and a Works Recreation Hall. We drilled in a stable too but as Wellington would have remarked that did not make us into horses.

I remember once being very roughly ejected from Maghera Orange Hall over some petty disagreement. To say that the Orange Order had any direct influence over the USC is bunkum. The force was under the Inspector General of RUC who answered to the Minister of Home Affairs. Sadly by the time Sir Arthur's book was out the Specials were part of history

In September 1969 Mr Wilson had the power in his hands and was not going to renege on his promise to the Republicans .

A Carson or a Brookborough with people power behind him might have saved the B Men at such a juncture. But even that is debatable.

An Oliver Cromwell might have used his well known dictum.

' *By the Bowels of Christ, Gentlemen,*
does it not occur to you that you might be wrong?. '

Had we but known it, Mr Wilson's act was in the words of Conor Cruise O'Brien an early step in Britain's effort ' *to tiptoe un-noticed away from Northern Ireland.* '

Parliamentary lack of fibre was to cause many thousand of deaths over the next quarter century and leave Ulster undefended against the ethnic cleansing of Protestants that was to follow the so- called Truce of 1994.

In Sept 1969 Colonel John Hunt of Everest climbing fame was beguiled into becoming a tool of the disbandment. He was given a month to make a Northern Ireland Security Review, a job that in the nineties took Chris Patton two years. Hunt's team of three were no doubt sincere in trying to create peace but quite out of their depth on such an assignment.

Harry Kennedy, Willie Beatty and I were interviewed midway by a weary Lord Hunt and his courteous henchmen, senior police officers men from London and Glasgow. The policemen were clearly influenced by the English dislike of any armed constabulary and gave the impression was that their minds were made up.

The inquiry indeed had the look of a burlesque. Asked a direct question Hunt assured me that he was not going to leave Ulster without an effective internal security force, even temporarily. His intentions were clear but to leave Ulster relatively undefended was exactly what his report was to do.

It was clear to any observer of Irish history that Hunt's report would be looked on as a huge Nationalist political success. And from it a major IRA military campaign would surely follow.

The publishing of the Report was not without its local prelude.

One of Maghera District's final jobs was the guarding of beautiful Moyola Park. Set beside the river of that name and surrounded by well treed lawns at Castledawson it was the home of the Prime Minister. There on 2nd October1969 the patrol commanded by Special Sergeant Fred Kyle of Innisrush was visited by Quintin Hogg (later Lord Hailsham), then Shadow Home Secretary. He was a man of the greatest distinction. with strong Ulster origins and had arrived to show my cousin James Chichester–Clark, the PM,. an advance copy of the Report. As a wartime Rifle Brigade officer Mr Hogg had just the right words to thank the B men for their record and the way they were still carrying out their duties.

The Report lay open and tantalising on the sofa in the Drawing Room but protocol forbade me being shown it.

. When later the public read the Hunt Report it contained very little criticism of the USC but confirmed its ' phasing out '. Paragraph 27 showed the limitations of Hunt's understanding, and the low quality of his briefing .

'…. a realistic assessment of the capacity of the IRA to mount serious terrorists attacks would not rate it very high, particularly as the Government of the Irish Republic has stated publicly that it opposed to the use of force on the Border'.

During the next few months gun running scandals in the Republic came to light involving the dismissal of two Government Ministers

As well as disbanding the B Specials Hunt's Report included the disarming of the Royal Ulster Constabulary . They were no longer to carry firearms, something they had found it essential to do for self protection since their formation in 1922 . The steel doors and shutters were to be removed from all RUC Stations.

Only after strong representations by the Ulster Government had the forming of a new security force been included. Two thousand strong it was to be recruited locally as part of the regular army under the control of the GOC Northern Ireland
. ie not the police or Stormont Government.

Two thousand men, mostly untrained, were supposed to take the place of twelve thousand Specials .

A shrewd old B man remarked to me, 'Them boys in the Government are like the owner of a big house in the Troubles saying to the family in his gate lodge, "Take the locks off your doors, throw away your weapons and I'll protect you." And then doing dang all about it. Once the B's is gone there'll be no one left to protect our wives and families '. He was right -- dead right you might almost say. But it all began to happen.

A Westminster White Paper confirmed that the disbandment of the Specials was to take place within six months.

IRA leaders exulted afresh at this double stroke of luck -- the RUC toothless and the B men on the way out. Foreseeing the long gap in security which would inevitably follow, the Godfathers swiftly made use of it to add to their weapons and manpower. They were to enjoy a golden opportunity to move around arms and explosives un-hampered, identify safe houses and establish caches. Recruit training began in thirty camps set up in the Republic. This was widely reported but the Government turned a deaf ear.

Our hearts sank but most B Men managed to swallow the disillusionment amounting to disgust felt at their treatment by Westminster. Fearing what would happen to the Province without them many joined the Ulster Defence Regiment, the last thing the Republicans had intended. The B's formed the backbone of the new force but the UDR grew slowly. Only 1600 strong at the time of becoming operational, the UDR had mustered just 3,700 six months later. It took until 1976 to peak at 9000. The IRA unwatched and uninhibited grew much faster.

Those of us who did join the UDR grew fond and proud of the regiment --- it did much brave and brilliant work but man for man or pound for pound sterling it never was anything like as effective as the Ulster Special Constabulary. It took so long in an emergency to call men in, issue weapons from an armoury, then send them back to set up check points where they had come from that the enemy almost invariably dispersed before the UDR could intercept them.

The USC should have had its retirement age trimmed to 55 and been given modern transport, weapons, equipment and training . This way it could been made ready in a fraction of the time and at a fraction of the cost that it took to form the UDR .

The RUC, with 20,000 B Men as a backup could have capped the IRA's campaigns for ever. That would have given politicians a chance to work out solutions without the appalling bloodshed of the seventies and eighties and the hatreds deepened by thousands of murders.

'Thon man should'a stuck to climbing mountains', was among the mildest of the opinions of Hunt by those B men and policemen who had to face the terrorists on the ground.

The Maghera District sadly prepared for what was to come Goodbyes were said to our full time staff and the District cups and trophies placed in ownership of a Trust. They are presently lodged in safe hands near Upperlands

On Sunday 22 March 1970 a Commemoration Service was held in the Kings Hall, Balmoral. It was one the most melancholy days of my public life.

Arthur Young, the new Inspector General seconded from London, appeared to have relished putting in place the disbandment. He was greeted on arrival with loud boohs. It was the B Men's sole sign, if you could call it that, of indiscipline.

There was no booh when The Prime Minister of Northern Ireland Major James Chichester Clark DL MP stood up to give the Address

> '*For you with your magnificent achievements, and for me – conscious as I am of all your service has meant to Ulster—today's occasion has elements of sadness . You have done magnificently, and will continue to do so .*
> *You have acted always, and will act to the last, as a loyal and disciplined force of patriotic Ulstermen.*
> *All down the years you have had much to endure –not only attacks of enemies of this State which you have beaten off time and again --but the insidious tactics of slur and innuendo. I have read with indignation some of the distorted accounts of your force which have appeared in Britain and elsewhere.*
> *Ulster owes you an immense debt – for the years of training, for the lonely hours on watch in desolate places at dead of night, for the courage and sense of duty which you have displayed, for the way that you kept alive the ideals of service and loyalty to Queen and Country* '.

He might have added that they were victims of the least endearing characteristic of British Governments in recent times - a tendency to sacrifice their friends to appease their enemies.

Each man later received a vellum certificate— one issued to my friend and colleague who typified the best sort of B Man read as follows -

ULSTER SPECIAL CONSTABULARY
1920-1970
For Loyal and Distinguished Service
This testimonial is awarded to
Special Sergeant James A.H. Crowe
on the stand down of the Force in recognition and appreciation of his
loyal and distinguished service in the Ulster Special Constabulary
to The Government and People of Northern Ireland

James Chichester Clark
Prime Minister
Stormont Northern Ireland

Let me here say that in 25 years service with the USC as a constable, sergeant and commandant I never witnessed any illegal behaviour, any physical abuse or anything done that I would have hesitated to have allowed to be fully publicized. We were ordinary law-abiding citizens who were prepared to turn out when needed to prevent terrorist attacks on our homes.

If there was an occasional bad man in some USC units, I can state positively that there were none in the Maghera District. Because so many words written about the B's have been twisted by the Queen's enemies to be used against them one must write with an unusual degree of care and this applies to the above comments which based on personal experience.

The Maghera District records of men and arms were meticulously kept and regularly inspected.

After the notice of disbandment the USC remained steadfast, doing guards until the last minute --only one Platoon, not a Derry one, handed in their weapons early. As B Men joined the UDR at the beginning of the new year we found ourselves, as Sergeant Roy Moore put it, 'in the both at the one time'.

And so we were.

But it was guards only we were used for. No positive anti- terrorist action took place in the final six months. How the IRA chortled.

On 31st March 1970 the USC handed in all weapons and equipment That may have surprised some people but the B men were a disciplined force . Some Districts, I was told only recently, were made to feel like criminals as the Army collected their weapons. This was not so in our case but it hurt our crack shots to see rifles that had been cared for like new-born babes and won prizes year after year in competition hurled roughly like scrap into a lorry.

I recall seeing a pile of peaked caps half filling a garage behind the Maghera Police Station. My heart was too full to go for a camera . But I wished afterwards that I'd made a photographic record.

A USC Association was soon formed which has done a fine job in keeping alive the tradition of virtually unpaid public service .

Once the B men had gone the chance of effective suppression of the IRA was almost doomed. My book *Brave Men and True* due out shortly will tell of the Maghera men's experience with me in the new force.

Many stayed in the UDR for over twenty years until it in turn in 1993 fell before another vicious and mendacious propaganda campaign which was widely believed in Britain.

Let Sir Arthur Hezlet have the last word on the appeasement-driven destruction of the USC.

'So went a Force of dedicated patriotic men whose only real crime was that they were all Protestants. They (the Specials) were prepared to take on a difficult and dangerous job for very little reward.. Far from being a political police force to oppress the minority the USC for 50 years protected Northern Ireland from many attempts to seize power by force against the wishes of the vast majority of the population'

Maghera District June 28th 1939

Upperlands Post June 1939

Tamlaght Post June 1939

Ballinahone Post June 1939

Tobermore Post June 1939

Culnady Post June 1939

Maghera Post June 1939

Evening Telegraph.

CO. DERRY "B" MEN.

PARADE AT UPPERLANDS.

ADDRESS BY COLONEL MACRORY.

On Wednesday evening the members of No. 2 District (County Derry) "B" Special Constabulary were the guests of Mr. H. F. Clark, District Commandant, and Mrs. Clark, at their residence, "Rockwood," Upperlands, County Derry.

The men paraded at the Recreation Hall, Upperlands, under their sub-district commandants, and headed by Upperlands Pipe Band, marched to Upperlands, where a saluting base had been erected. The salute was taken by Colonel Macrory, D.L., D.S.O., County Commandant.

Addressing the gathering Colonel Macrory said he had met many of them on a number of previous occasions, both at musketry and patrol duty. On the latter occasions he had been held up with great determination, but also with great courtesy, and that was exactly as it should be. As they knew, they would be giving up patrol duty at the end of that week, and from July 1 they, in common with the entire "B" Force, would enter what was known as the drill category. He knew there was a widespread feeling of reluctance towards that change, but he would ask every officer and man to suppress that feeling and to show the same spirit of devotion to duty which had always characterised them. He would ask them to remember that there was a national emergency and the "B" Force, trained and disciplined, he was certain, would, prove a not unworthy successor to the Ulster Volunteer Force, which formed the nucleus of the world-famous Ulster Division.

The "B" men and other visitors, numbering about 400, were entertained to tea by Mr. and Mrs. H. F. Clark.

Col. Macrory expressed cordial thanks to Mr. Clark for his hospitality and kindness. In Mr. Clark they had an officer who would always look after their interests and help them in every way possible. He would also like to thank Mrs. Clark for her great kindness to them.

Mr. Clark said it gave Mrs. Clark and himself much pleasure to have their guests that evening and he felt sure that the same enthusiasm which was manifested by the men on patrol duty would again be evident when the drill category came into operation.

Belfast Telegraph June 1939

Stand Down Parade of the Ulster Home Guard, Magherafelt 1944.
The right marker, Platoon Sergeant Jim Crowe, was like many Home Guardsmen also a member of the USC . Figures at right: Lt Jim Clark, Major Joe Burns, Major Willie Clark.

Working Party of B Men have a stand easy while tidying up the surrounds.
Left to Right: Constables T Rogers, A Clark, J Steele, D Linton, Ivan Patterson,
Sergeant Instructor John Chestnut, Constables N Clarke, R Paul, and W Linton.

The New Drill Hut, Maghera, 1965

Major James Chichester Clark, Prime Minister of Northern Ireland

Commemoration Service for the Ulster Special Constabulary in the Kings Hall Belfast.
March 1970. Front row:Lord Brookeborough, Lord Glentoran,Lady Glentoran,
The Duke of Abercorn, Lady Pym,
Back row:Hon. John and Mrs Brooke, Inspector General Arthur Young.

Lt. Colonel Bobby Scott, Londonderry County Commandant

'Making the rafters ring' at a USC Supper in the Factory Dining Hall Upperlands. Colonel Ken Davidson - County Commandant, Harry Clark -retired District Commandant and John Chestnut, Robby Hessin, SDC. John Patterson

Mr. Quintin Hogg, Shadow Home Secretary, talks to Sergeant Fred Kyle of Innishrush in charge of the USC guard at Moyola Lodge on the eve of the publication of the Hunt report. Robin Chichester- Clark, Westminister MP for Londonderry is in the background.

District Commandants Willie Beatty, Wallace Clark MBE, DL, and Harry Davidson MBE, ERD, at the Kings Hall 22 March 1970

No. 71368

Not transferable.

RESTORATION OF ORDER IN IRELAND REGULATIONS.

SPECIAL MOTOR PERMIT FOR ONE JOURNEY ONLY.

Mr. *Alex. W. Clark, D.L., J.P.* of *Upperlands, Co. Derry*
who is the holder of Ordinary Permit No. *26002* in respect of Motor Vehicle No. *I.W. 892* is hereby exempted from the restrictions imposed upon the use of motor vehicles in Ireland to the following extent :—

(1). He may use the said motor vehicle between the hours of *6am & 11pm* on *Friday 10th June 1921* and ~~~~~~~ on ~~~~~~~

(2). He may between the above-mentioned hours proceed in the said motor vehicle by the most direct route between his place of residence or garage as shown on the said ordinary permit, and *Belfast*, and may return therefrom to the said place of residence or garage.

(3). He may between the above-mentioned hours garage the said motor vehicle at any garage where motor vehicles are authorised to be kept for hire, provided that he shall forthwith give notice to the nearest police or military barracks that he has garaged the said vehicle at the said garage, and shall produce this permit and his ordinary permit.

DATE *9. 6. 21*

SINGLE JOURNEY

OFFICE OF
DISTRICT INSPECTOR
R/C
C. F. N. MACREADY,
COMPETENT MILITARY AUTHORITY.

NOTE.—(1). This permit must be returned to the Office of Issue immediately it has expired.
(2). The motor vehicle in respect of which this permit is issued must be immediately stopped at the request of any policeman or soldier and this permit together with the holder's ordinary permit must be produced for inspection.
(3). If the motor vehicle in respect of which this permit is issued is used otherwise than in accordance with the provisions of any Order restricting the use of motor vehicles in Ireland as modified by this permit, the motor vehicle will be liable to be forfeited, and the holder of this permit will be liable in addition to heavy penalties.

[OVER.